For The Love of Christian Homemaking

Books by Mrs. White

Mother's Faith

For The Love of Christian Homemaking

Cover Photo: Mrs. White's Parlour in Vermont

Mother Was Here

My grandbaby kept me very busy today. Sometimes, he will play happily on a quilt, or in his little seat. Then I can do the dishes, or start a load of laundry. We all take turns holding him while someone makes supper, a snack, or cleans up a mess. We work in the middle of the joy, of this blessing of a baby in our home.

This afternoon, no one was around while I took care of baby and kept house. The kitchen had its noon mess, waiting for attention. While the baby played, I deep- cleaned the stove top and one of the counters. These two areas were spotless, while the other half of the kitchen was neglected. But those clean sections brought me great happiness. Looking at them, sent a precious message to say, "*Mother was Here*."

Years ago, my father used to joke about our childhood home. He said the house was such a mess that if the police had come, they wouldn't know if there had "been a struggle." For the life of me, I cannot remember our house even slightly messy. This must have happened when we were all babies and toddlers. *But it is fun to imagine* my very neat mother with a messy house. She knew what was most important. I am sure she had clean spots in her house that sent the *bless-ed* message that, "*Mother was Here.*"

We all know that babies don't keep. Lately, I spend most of my time sitting by the window, in my grandmother's old rocking chair, holding her great-great grandson, and wondering how happy she must be, smiling down at us from heaven.

Each Mother, in each generation, leaves legacies, memories, creations and sweet lessons. Their diligent work in the home, *and their caring for babies*, is their greatest accomplishment in life.

How precious is the comforting evidence in our daily lives, that "*Mother was here.*"

The Duties of Home

In hospitals, "housekeeping" comes in each morning and cleans the rooms. Trash is removed, the floor is swept, the room is disinfected and everything is put back to "rights." These same tasks are *duties* that must be done in the home. However, *sadly*, housework today is often neglected because our mentality of "freedom," catering to our moods, and the idea that chores are to be done on a flexible schedule (in other words: *when one feels like it*).

Honestly, I fight with this attitude myself. It is a daily battle. But we *must* do our sweeping and our washing and our cleaning and our cooking; all at routine, *expected* times. This brings order in the home. It brings stability, and it keeps things pleasant and clean.

The best way to do this is to make it a *habit*. There should be morning duties. There should be afternoon tasks, and evening work. This is a highly valuable job and it should be done with pride, *despite* our lazy moods. I am as much to blame as anyone else! Underneath it all, I have the mindset of an entitled, pampered, slacker. (gentle smiles) This is why I often have to set a "mood" to clean and keep house.

I have to turn on a sermon, or old gospel music, on my kitchen radio. I have to light candles, fluff pillows, and straighten the drapes before I can start anything. Once I commence my work, I love it! I love to vacuum carpets, polish furniture, shine mirrors and do dishes by the back window. The hard part, for most of us, is just putting down the cup of tea, setting aside a good book, and getting out of a comfortable parlour chair to do the chores.

Only Rich People Have Clean Houses

"Our homes should be neat with a swept sidewalk leading to the front door." - Emilie Barnes

Have you ever thought that only rich people have clean homes? When we consider the idea of poverty, we imagine dingy, dirty, tenement homes and people wearing tattered garments. It is the image of being in dire straits with no money for soap or the basic necessities of life.

As we work in our humble homes, we must not have dirty surroundings. It is not only the rich who have clean homes. While they do have servants and housekeepers and fine things - we have our own labor, and we must take pride in a job well done. We are like the *Hebrew women* spoken of in Scripture (by the midwives) who were strong and hard working; unlike Pharaoh's Egyptian women who lived a life of ease. We can *most certainly* find a little time, each day, to tend to our homes.

A clean and neat home makes it a welcoming place. But we must make the effort to *work*. Doing dishes, sweeping floors, doing laundry - these are all necessary tasks. I read about this elderly aunt who walked into the home of her grown niece. The niece was the mother to 5 children. She was an excellent housekeeper. Well, on this particular day, she had a sink full of dishes and other housework she needed to do. But the Aunt found her resting in bed. She thought, perhaps she was ill, or expecting another child. She said, **"Why else would you be laying down when there is work to be done?"** I have thought of that statement on many occasions. I would sit in my parlour chair and start to read a book, but remember those wise words. It would startle me into being responsible. I would clean my kitchen first. Then I would sit down for my break.

It is a precious feeling, knowing I have a home I can make into a lovely place. *Yet I must do the work.*

The Light in the Window

It is so dark and stormy outside. My house feels *cold* and *empty*. It seems like the days are getting shorter. It makes people sad, like there is a depression falling over our homes.

One thing I like do to is turn on a few lamps in the early afternoon. It sends a gentle light throughout the house. Those driving by, or walking by our house, will see a light in the window. They will see that someone is home. . . That someone cares about this place. . They will see that light, and feel welcomed and warmed.

It's time for me to turn on a quiet CD of songs by Frank Sinatra and Bing Crosby. I will turn on my kitchen lamp, put on my apron, and start cleaning.

Soon it will be time for the early evening's errands. I will have to go out. But before I do, I want to make sure everything is *neat* and *pleasant* and *happy*. Mr. White will have the wood stove on, for when I come home later. I will see the pretty light in the window, and feel welcomed **in my own home** as I walk through the door.

I don't want to have that bad feeling when I come home tonight - the one of *dread*, because I left the house without cleaning first. I want to come home to *order* and *beauty*. . . and a little lamplight to make me smile.

Desperate For 10 Minute Cleanings

Throughout the day, I look for opportunities to clean. I might wash a few dishes, straighten an afghan, sweep a floor, or tidy a bookcase. These little touches help keep the house in order.

When things get really busy at home, with activities, the needs and troubles of children, and the constant care of the very young, there is little time for housework.

If I gave up and just let all the work go, my house would be an **embarrassing shambles**. There would be no excuse. I would be utterly ashamed of myself! This is why I love to take 10 minutes here-and-there, throughout the day, to clean and organize. If I keep up with things, in this way, and a catastrophe hits, it is okay to stop my work and tend to other duties without my house looking like a filthy unkempt home.

We mothers need to be proud of our homes and our work at home. If we don't take pride in our work, we will not give our best effort.

Sometimes our moods will interfere with our ability to work. When this happens, it's time to bring in rainbows and happiness. Whatever ambiance you can create to help you get to work, would help tremendously. Sometimes I listen to Bing Crosby singing Christmas songs! Other times, some gospel or classical music is what I need. I also love to clear off the kitchen table and light a candle. *I then clean around the prettiness I just created.* Your mood will seriously affect your work ethic. Don't let sadness, annoyances, worries or laziness take away your pride of a neat house.

The grounds of our homes, the front porch, the entryway, and all the rooms inside, give an image of the type of hospitality and love that comes from our family. It must be neat and inviting. This takes a *cheerfulness*, and a *willingness*, and a love of HOME.

Beware of Random Kitchen Inspections

I scrubbed and cleaned out my fridge and freezer last night. As I worked, I remembered kitchens of yesteryear. .

We used to have a variety of colors for refrigerators. There was cream, yellow, green or white. I've also seen country red and blue in pictures. I remember our fridges were mostly a cheery yellow. (*I have never liked the sterile, cold look of stainless steel that is presented as a modern necessity.*)

Refrigerators needed to be cleaned once each week. This would be a deep cleaning, which included throwing out unused leftovers and discarding old produce. We would also get a big bucket, cloth and towel. We would use hot water and a cleaning product and start scrubbing every inch of the fridge shelves, walls, drawers and door. Then we would dry and polish it all.

Some refrigerators had to be defrosted. In this case, it was turned off, emptied out, and given time for all the built - up ice to melt into a special pan. Then we would get in there and clean the whole thing out. This was also done on a weekly basis.

A clean fridge was just part of a clean kitchen. It was normal work we all expected to do.

Years ago, I remember a mother who was setting up her home as a daycare. She was told that she could enroll in a food program, which would provide checks to reimburse her for the meals she provided to the children. But she was *worried* because the worker would come into her home, *randomly*, and **inspect** her refrigerator and oven. Why would that bother her? Was it because she was not keeping things clean?

Can you imagine if someone randomly came by and inspected our kitchens?

Sometimes I think about this. Before I sit down to rest in the evenings, I go in my kitchen and tidy things up. When I notice my fridge is not orderly, I like to do a quick clean up and make things look neat. This is one of the many things that keep a housewife occupied and productive. This also helps keep a sanitary home.

After we make lunch or dinner, I notice a piled up mess. This becomes the challenge. The best thing to do is get in there promptly and get the work finished. There are going to be messes. And that is okay. That is part of life. But we cannot neglect the cleaning part. . . Top chefs have been trained to make delicious food, **and** run a sanitary, clean environment. They also have random checks by the health department. They are graded, on a point scale, based on cleanliness. They are always proud to get 100% scores or an "A."

If you were given 30 minutes notice, would you get an "A" for a clean kitchen?

But here is the sad part.... what about those who don't care if they get an "F"? Why don't we have more people take pride in a clean kitchen, like the Top Chefs and the Mothers of yesteryear?

Making Room for Life

A year or two ago, I packed up hundreds of books and donated them to my local library. The books were taking over and they had to go! I went through a major withdrawal period, thinking I "lost" books I would need later. But eventually I forgot about them.

This is happening again. More and more books have entered my home. They are in my "dressing room," the hall bookcase, and the bedrooms. It is too much. I hate to let more go, but I will pack some up today and give them to the library.

I need to make room for living. I want an uncluttered home. I will keep only those books (and items) that are meaningful for me on a daily basis. I realize it will be painful, but this type of de-cluttering must be done consistently, in order to keep our home pleasant and functioning.

Many years ago, I visited the beautiful old home of a neighbor. She was a retired teacher in her 80's. She showed me her home library. She had plenty of rooms, and this library was elegant and lovely. Her collection of books were old, but important to her. *She said we should **never** get rid of our books.* Her wisdom sometimes gives me guilt when I want to de-clutter. But I know that if I only get rid of books that are "fluff" or not important to me, then I am not necessarily getting rid of them, but sharing them with others, while making room in my home for what matters to me most.

So today, I will vacuum and sweep and clean my kitchen. I will do laundry and homeschool. But my main project of the day will be to fill up a couple of bags full of old books and get them out of the house before I change my mind. I want pleasant rooms in this house, and this mission is essential to our happiness.

When Cooking and Cleaning is Too Much

I've gotten into the habit lately of cleaning without cooking. I do dishes and polish the kitchen two or three times a day. I have a little help, but mostly enjoy the work alone, while listening to sermons, or gospel, on my kitchen radio. It is a peaceful, happy time, working in the kitchen. I also keep the other rooms neat and do most of the laundry. I enjoy this work very much.

But if I add cooking the meals to that? It would overwhelm me. My teenagers have taken over the cooking for now. Amy (17) often makes the lunches or suppers. John (15) makes tea, snacks and some of the meals. Matt (19) will occasionally make a meal for us all, but mostly makes himself something easy to eat very quickly, since he is on a busy schedule. Mr. White makes a big breakfast in the early morning hours, each day. Whoever is awake gets to enjoy a hearty meal with him. But we are all mostly asleep at that time!

As the cold weather is approaching our rural Vermont town, I will want to start making beef stew with biscuits, or lasagna and Italian bread. But first I must build up my strength and get some energy. To cook **and** to clean when one is often weary can be too much!

The other afternoon, I sat in my parlour chair with a nice book. Matthew was in the kitchen making an early dinner. He brought me some ginger-ale. I was delighted! The more rest we mothers get, the more work we are able to do *pleasantly*.

To do my work in a slow-paced manner, I have to have plenty of helpers. Children and teenagers have a tremendous amount of energy. They can sweep a floor, take out the trash, clean a bathroom, sweep a porch, do dishes, cook meals and many other things very quickly! But I wouldn't want them to do *everything*. I would feel left out of the fun of housework!

So I rest as much as I can, doing enjoyable things - like reading or watching an old movie. I also love to *visit* with the family in the parlour. I consider my housework my "breaks" from my "rest." I can spend much more time resting, and doing what I want, if my **breaks** are the chores. (It's kind of like rushing through doing dishes during a commercial.)

Simplicity of Old Fashioned Homemaking

We've all seen the busy housewife, who decorates and bakes and throws delightful parties. She shops and she plans. She is so active in, an out of, the home, that many look at her and wonder where she gets her energy. Most observe her life and despair of trying to mimic her! She is her own star and she is unreachable!

There is another way. It is the humble, basic way of simplicity. It might look meager and poor. It might even look too easy. But this way can be obtained by far more housewives, if they only realize it is *okay* to be simple.

There is a slowness to it. . . **There is no ambition**. . . It is the quiet servant - *the meek one*, who guides the home.

This housewife putters around the house and yard, cleaning and cooking in her own way.

In the old days, oatmeal or porridge was the morning meal. Perhaps some bread and butter went with it. No family was served processed, sugary cereal because it had not yet been invented. Now today, can you imagine serving morning guests some oatmeal? How many would balk at it? But it is healthy and nourishing and warm and comforting!

A simple lunch of baked beans and biscuits with hot tea might be served during the afternoon break from chores. This isn't a takeout meal, or a fast food lunch. It isn't an elaborate planned out menu item. It was what was available in the pantry.

Domestic occupations were not about planning elaborate events for the home. The simple duties were for the comfort of the family and basic survival. The laundry, the sweeping, the mopping, the cooking, the dusting were all on the normal agenda at home. The homemaker would put on her housedress and apron and be "on duty" for the day. She was there to tend to the home and family. She was not the 'event planner' or the one to spoil the children by gratifying their every worldly "want."

There is something very basic and very lovely about an old time homelife. Bible reading and family prayers were done morning and evening. The family would have afternoon prayers with the noon meal. They would break from their labor to worship the Lord. *Thoughts of heaven, eternal rest and joy were the ambition.* The focus was on the journey home and the blessed example they could leave to those around them.

Many of us crave this kind of life, but we are often tripped up and confused by what goes on in our culture. A routine of homelife, the act of ironing or washing floors in the quiet of the morning (while praying or singing old time hymns) can help keep us grounded. Are we not pilgrims and strangers on this earth? May the Lord help us avoid acting like the "stars" of this world.

The Mother Who Isn't Busy

Serving a family and keeping a home takes a lot of time. Doing it peacefully, without much else to occupy the energy, will leave a lasting impression.

When Mother is available all day long, for whatever needs arise, she is cherished and counted on. Can you imagine the mother who wants to see her family fed and full and happy, and who enjoys making snacks and meals for her loved ones? Imagine she never says, *"just a minute. I have to finish my own thing first."*

Imagine this same mother spending time with each family member, doing what *they* enjoy. Imagine her going outside with the teen boys and cheering them on in their games. Imagine her chatting with her girls and doing projects *they* want to do. Imagine her sitting in the parlour chair, serving tea, and happily getting up to serve someone in need.

She can't do any of this, **cheerfully**, *unless she isn't busy.*

This mother will find great peace and contentment in serving her family. Notice, she is not the slave. She is not the doormat.

She is greatly esteemed, respected and dearly loved. She is NEEDED and wanted. Her children and husband seek her out for help, comfort, and her presence because they know they are her entire world. *They* are her hobby, her project, her joy.

Yet, she will deal with moods and messes. She learns to handle them with grace and dignity. She will guide the characters of those in her charge, and she will do it sweetly. Her example of patient, methodical work with a cheerful attitude (despite trials or tears) will pour inspiration and love into their minds and hearts.

And if she ever has those overwhelmed moments, or faces difficulties, she will go into her prayer closet and get help from the one who knows all and sees all. She will get her comfort there, and she will be renewed and ready to joyfully get back to *her life of not being busy.*

Sometimes, when we strive to do our own thing, the real thing we are destined to do gets neglected and trampled over.

The greatest goal of a mother and wife, is to dedicate her days to the lifetime vocation of home and family.

Security of Home Routines

On weekend mornings, my father would listen to old country gospel music in the kitchen while he and Mother made breakfast for us all. We children were teenagers and would sleep as late as we could. They would make a big pancake breakfast and it had such a delightful scent. It was a lovely way for us all to wake up.

Dad worked hard as a laborer. He kept a solid, predictable, calm routine in the home. We knew he would be watching westerns on Saturday afternoons. We knew he would be in the garage working on a project, or fixing the family cars. He did yard work and kept a garden. He also came home from work at the same time every day. Looking back at his life, **HE** was what kept things steady, no matter what was going on in our family.

Parents are like guardian angels. They are there to guide and watch over their children. But they do not get burned, or harmed, or pulled down, into their children's troubles. They are unscathed and strong. This helps build up courage in our children. This teaches them, as they mature in this life.

Our routines in the home are what keep things safe and secure. If our children (old or young) are struggling in this life, and they see Mother and Father cooking *like always*, or cleaning *like always*, or putting away the dinner dishes, *like always*, the children are comforted. On the other hand, if Mother and Father stop all they normally do and indulge in despair, and dwell on the trials so that it cripples the routine, the entire family is brought down.

Tonight, as I turn on the lamp light in the parlour, and sit in my favorite chair to do my Prentiss study*, my children will feel a sense of security. As we finish up our evening routine and smile the smile of peace, and contented joy, despite any hidden tears, the children will feel the warmth and love of home. And they will heal from whatever harm the world has tried to cause. **Somehow, home and family will prevail**.

" The Prentiss Study" is an old fashioned Bible Study, available for free at The Legacy of Home blog.

Knowing When to Quit

Homemaking is an endless occupation. There are chores and errands and cooking to do. We also have our own ideas for projects and hobbies. I am often overwhelmed to the point that I have to force myself to sit down.

Today I thought about making a new dress, starting a knitting project, catching up on some book reading and baking some muffins. I had so many ideas racing through my mind that all I could do was sit at the table, look at my son (John) and say, *"I am bored."* How could that be? Because I was so overwhelmed with my plans that *I couldn't do anything.* I finally played a game of "Charlie Brown" Yahtzee with John so I could get my mind to stop and relax. (The pictures on the dice made us smile, and cheered me up!)

Pacing myself is one of the hardest of trials in my life at home. I did manage to clean several rooms, go out on an errand, read, make a nice lunch and bake a cake. Finally, late this afternoon, I decided that it was time to quit. It was time to be finished for the day. It was time to stop doing anything and just be at peace.

My evening will be one of relaxing. I will enjoy hobbies at my own pace and listen to classical music. I will light a lilac - scented candle and knit, or hand-sew, in my cozy parlour. I will drink tea and not worry about anything.

Just a little while ago, I told my youngest child (age 15), *we are finished for the day.* No more chores. Everything is perfectly neat. If it gets messed up in the next few hours, we will just leave it for the morning. He was delighted! He was off duty from helping me and I was off duty from housework (and of nagging for help! - smiles)

Sometimes, one of the greatest secrets of joyful homemaking is knowing when to quit.

A Humble Parlour as a School of Theology

It has been said that *Mothers of old time* spent their leisure hours reading the Bible to their children. These Mothers also lived a moral and virtuous life. The greatest witness of true character and holiness, are the eyes of the immediate family.

When Mother's hobby and devotion revolves *entirely* around the home, she has the freedom and the privilege of training her children in godliness.

(Do we realize that this is why mothers are being pulled away from the hearth?)

I remember when my children were little. The main part of their education was Scripture. We did not *focus* on memorizing some verses. We did not do *short* devotions or read *little* devotional books. We, the children from the age of solid readers (5 and up) and I, read the entire Bible over and over again, year after year after year.

We also had some help. . .

If the children didn't know the meaning of a word, we looked to the 1800's Webster's Dictionary. This is an enormous, hardcover book that cost me well over $60. It has thousands of pages. The children greatly respected this treasured resource.

If a phrase or passage confused me or the children, we looked to Matthew Henry. Or we used the Strong's Concordance. Later, we also added John MacArthur's study Bible to help answer our questions.

But the daily, hour by hour, readings took place using the trusty old KJV Bible. The children sharpened their minds with those "antiquated" words. They sharpened their reading skills and committed to memory (from repetitive reading) many precious truths.

As most of my children have grown up, I have heard and seen how they have faced "giants" of confusing doctrine. I have seen them stand their ground against unbiblical religions and people trying to convince them of another way. And each time, these children have prevailed and stood strong, as the strongest roots of an ancient oak tree. . . *Unbending and sure of their Faith.* While these children still struggle with their sin nature (as we all will until we reach the heavenly gates), nothing can sway them away from the lessons learned in the old parlour. Why? Because they learned sacred, ancient truths, that have stood the test of time.

The other day, I was sitting at the parlour table. I had my books and Bible laid out before me. One of my teenagers came by and wanted to read with me. We looked through Scripture and looked to our "helpers" to understand passages. And we delighted in spending valuable, fleeting time, on that which was eternal.

Our home may be old, with ripped up linoleum and cracks in the walls. The furnishings may be torn and "dated." We may have plain, inexpensive foods to share. We may have a poor income. But the time spent in my humble parlour, *in my school of theology,* is the greatest place this Mother could ever be.

Laboring Despite Weariness

I have often marveled at the reserves of energy my tired husband seems to have. He will drink coffee in the early evening so he can be awake to finish a few more chores. I couldn't understand why he didn't just sleep and forget the extra work.

In the last few weeks, I have been overly busy with my older children. I hosted a baby shower, had guests in my home at all times of the day, went to several events, did heavy shopping, and extra cleaning. Somehow, I got stronger and learned to pace myself enough to get it all done. I pushed aside distractions and wouldn't allow myself to be pulled away from the task at hand.

My goal is to make the most of my time as a mother. (How long do I really have left?) I want to make events special, and my home a happy haven. This all takes a tremendous amount of behind-the-scenes labor, which is seemingly unnoticed. Lately, I have done this all cheerfully, and have been thrilled with my daily accomplishments.

I also noticed this working in other areas of our life. I have daily Bible time with my teenage son (he is my last homeschool student). John and I read two chapters at each reading.

However, sometimes life gets in the way, and our time is delayed. Last night, it had gotten so late, I mentioned that perhaps we should read only one chapter? *He gave me such a look.* Like I was a slacker (smiles). And said almost sternly, almost accusingly, "Why can't we read two?" I was grateful for his persistence and we read the required two chapters. We were both proud of ourselves, realizing that if we had all day for other things, why on earth would we skip the daily religious disciplines?

My children watch Mr. White and I work hard on a daily basis. They see us quietly laboring without complaint. They watch as we do difficult things despite weariness. They also see us enjoy our rest and the fruit of our labor. This example in life, and in religious duties, helps our children learn to work despite the hard times. It teaches them to persevere, but to also come alongside and help us when we start failing.

If I gave in to my "tiredness" and slept as much as I wish I could, what kind of life would I be portraying to those around me? To work hard each day, and yes to **earn my rest**, is one of the best examples I can give to my children.

The Respite Before Church

A loud sermon played on the CD radio in my kitchen. I washed the dishes, swept the floor and polished the stove. I listened to spiritually **quickening** nourishment, while I tidied the parlour. Then I heard the church bells ring. I knew it would be time to leave soon.

There is a short time between daily tasks and religious duties that are like a "respite" for the soul. It is when we prepare for the unseen joy of seeking holiness.

Yet, if we left the house a mess, or did not prepare in advance to take care of our earthly work, oh how *restless* and *distracted* we would be during the church time!

We can slowly walk away from our work, knowing it was well done. We take a break from the world, and head to the sacred time of heavenly things. *Is this a foreshadowing of things to come?*

Some preparation time is necessary. If we are having a quiet Bible time at home, we gather our Bible and books and papers. We settle ourselves in our usual place before we begin. This is part of the respite. This is all part of the expectation and the eagerness, during the break between earthly and heavenly matters.

If we are to attend church and must travel, the time we get ready, or walk or drive is the respite. It is a time of contemplation, and a readiness, to rid of us worldly thoughts, so we can focus on better things.

I wonder if those few moments before mortal death, the saints feel a blissful peace as they enter their *long-awaited* home in the heavenly realm?

Mother's Rest

Small children must have naps, and a bedtime. They need a routine that helps protect their health, nerves, and well-being. We take excellent care of our little ones, but spoil *ourselves* with too much indulgence. In this modern world, we Mothers are sleeping less than ever. We are so occupied with a great many distractions. This is taking away our ability to have sufficient rest.

When I was a child, we had never heard of VCRs or DVD players. If we watched the one television set that was in our home (other than the small, portable for when someone was ill), we turned it off at a certain hour. Our parents went to bed at the same time each night. We children had our own bedtimes as well.

In Grandmother's day, the electricity was only used minimally. No one would dream of using the lights, or other items, late into the night unless there was some kind of emergency. The radio (if the family had one) was shut off at a certain time. Families would read together, visit, knit, play the piano, or play games. It used to be that when the streetlights came on, it was time to wind down the day. Families had dinner, clean up, and a short break in the living room. Bedtime soon followed.

Lately, I have been so guilty of not getting enough rest. I am staying up far too late because there is so much to occupy my time and thoughts. This is making me less productive! This is taking away some peaceful joy.

Sufficient sleep is a necessity, and we mothers must have a routine, just like the children.

The Pleasant Task of Cleaning

I often walk into a messy room and sigh. . . Yet I realize that if I don't use my creativity, the room will not look inviting. I want my rooms to be pretty. I want my husband and children to enjoy the *quiet* and *order* of home life.

All I have to do is put away a few items. . . Then tuck in chairs. . . I straighten pillows. . . sweep floors, and wash mirrors. Each little task is progress. Just another polish here, and a tidy there, and soon my rooms look lovely.

A messy room can be a challenge. But more often than not, it is a beautiful way for us to enjoy the fruit of our labor. With our own efforts and skills, we can create loveliness.

Once the work is done, I sit with a cup of tea and enjoy a much deserved homemaking break. But the greatest reward of all, is when my family walks into a room, smiles to themselves and does not say anything about it. They are content and at peace, because that is the environment I strive to keep for them.

Everything is right with the world, when Mother's home is pleasant and tidy.

The Comfort of a Dressing Room

Years ago, before we bought our 1800's house, I toured all the rooms. There are 14 on 3 floors. I was delighted with every new room we came across.

Off beyond the largest bedroom, was a dressing room. It looked like a sewing room, with an old singer on a table, and a rod (up above) for hanging clothes. There was also a pretty window overlooking the landscape.

It is now my dressing room. Beside the window is my grandmother's rocking chair. There are bookcases on an entire side wall for my personal library. I have a sturdy antique desk, which holds my collection of the writings of John Wesley. I also have notes, papers and research in a file box for later use. A large filing cabinet holds decades of my writings, household memorabilia, and other necessary files. This cabinet even holds a copy of Great - Grandfather's ordination certificate when he became a minister.

This room holds my sewing supplies in a drawer. There is yarn, knitting supplies and patterns in a large old bureau.

On a wall is a Bulletin Board presenting photographs, newspaper clippings of our home and our children (during their famous moments), and special notes, or cards that make me smile when I see them.

This is the room where I hide cases of ginger-ale so the children don't drink it all in one day. It is where I can sit quietly, listening to a sermon on the radio, while I rock in grandmother's chair by the window.

I spent many hours in this room, in 2007, as I recorded my voice onto tapes from a small vintage collection of puritan books for sermonaudio.com. * Grandfather set up a large radio and cassette player, along with a microphone for me. (I read from old books onto tapes and mailed them to the company so they could use them on their site.) I still remember looking out the window when I took breaks.

This is the room where I can decide what I will wear for church, a trip to the store, or to just keep home for the day.

This special room is like my own studio dressing room, where I can take a break, and prepare for each day, or retreat to in the evening hours.

Studios provide actresses with their own dressing rooms. This is where they can relax and take a break before working hard at their craft. Even young actors received dressings rooms. Shirley Temple had one and was kept protected from fans and the hectic atmosphere of working on a set. This is where she rested, and where she studied.

To have something like a Dressing Room in our own home is a luxury. Some of us can have one in the Parlour, a bedroom, or a small den. Others may have an extra room they can convert into a special sanctuary where Mother can have her lovely things, or supplies.

In the old days, many Fathers had dens. This was a mixture of a home office and a library. Children were respectful of this room and in awe of their Fathers.

Mothers have always had a corner of the house for their special things. A comfortable dressing room is a lovely blessing for which I am grateful.

* I did this work for them, in exchange for free books.

The Morning Work

The sun has not yet risen. . . The house is quiet. . . **There is pleasant work waiting for me**. . . I turned on the parlour heater and will start polishing and cleaning before my family wakes up.

I will turn on some quiet classical music (Mozart) and I will work by lamp-light. It will be a lovely morning of work.

When the family wakes up, all will be clean and neat. . . all will be well. Their morning moods will not phase me, because I will have been in **the quiet sanctuary of a godly home**. I will be prepared with the armor of kindness, patience, endurance, and I will be full of a *slow* and *sweet* temper.

This will happen because of the seclusion of my morning work.

Some rise early to run, exercise, or go to the gym. But this housewife rises early for the precious joy of keeping the home.

Peacefully Occupied

Can you imagine if we were not in a big hurry, or always late? Each day, we mostly have the same routine. We know what is expected of us. So why do we rush around and have a difficult time? Why are we stressed out and feeling overwhelmed?

I venture to say it is because we are not being efficient or methodical.

It is so important to have a variety of projects going on in the home. We can get bored very easily if we only have housework to do. We need to make decorating plans, and occasionally re-arrange rooms to make them fresh and cheerful.

Simple tasks like sweeping a porch or removing weeds from the front property can be pleasant outdoor work because we can enjoy some quiet and fresh air.

Doing some late afternoon ironing to get a pretty outfit ready for the next day will keep us from being rushed.

Efficiency can be used during housework by combining other tasks at the same time. When on the phone - clean out a purse, or peel potatoes. When cleaning the living room, wear (light) ankle weights for an extra boost of exercise. When removing clutter from a desk or counter, watch a little educational television or listen to pleasant music.

Keep to a standard routine. Meals should be at certain hours. Heavy chores should happen at specific times. Eventually, they will be common and memorized, and seem to happen on their own.

If we make homemaking the focus of our lives, the one thing we **master** and do well, we are more likely to be peaceful, and less likely to be distracted.

An expert at something is confident and peaceful. But it takes a lot of practice to get there. At first there will be mistakes and clumsiness. But if we keep at it, eventually we will be occupied at home in a way that is greatly admired. This will also bring us a tremendous amount of pride in our daily work.

Inspired to Keep House

I used to receive some lovely old fashioned magazines in the mail. These were mostly homemade or published by small companies. They focused on Motherhood and Homemaking. There were also many charming books on these subjects that supported and encouraged wives in their work at home.

Writings in these publications on subjects like cookery, mothering, housekeeping, and being a sweet and good wife were like honey to soothe the soul.

The covers were beautifully decorated with pretty gardens, handmade quilts, home canned jams and other such enticing photographs or illustrations.

Before these periodicals were around, we wives depended on our church friends, family and our memories to help us along the way. We were taught the home arts by Mother and grandmother. This was when it was more common for women to stay at home and pass on the skills to the next generation.

When a grand-baby was expected, mother leaned on grandma for gentle support, advice and encouragement. The extended family taught skills of child care, patience, grace and the beauty of being home, by a *living example,* and by loving support.

The old ways are tried and true paths of peace. The greatest thing we mothers learned by the older generation was to ride out the storms of life without giving up. We learned endurance, and how to stand strong and tall, following the principles of godly living, **no matter what was happening around us**.

This is what keeps the old paths alive. We don't walk away. We don't look at other options.

We must constantly strive to perfect the peace and comfort we can give to those in our midst with our godly hospitality. This is what helps inspire the next generation to keep house.

Renewing the Mind for Motherhood

"You are as much serving God in looking after your own children, and training them up in God's fear, and minding the house, and making your household a church for God, as you would be if you had been called to lead an army to battle for the Lord of Hosts." - Charles Spurgeon

Dear Mothers,

Don't let the world distract you away from the most important job you will ever have. Don't let them pull you away with promises of money, fame and good times.

Here, in our humble homes, little by little and bit by bit, our quiet, steady influence in the home will impact society and succeeding generations. But it takes *years* and *years* to see the results. It takes toiling and tears and patience.

Mothers, don't give up. Joy will certainly come on resurrection morning.

Summer Housekeeping

My husband and I both grew up in humble beach houses, in Massachusetts. For us, summer time always felt like a vacation. We can have this same feeling, even if we don't live near a beach.

Here in the mountains of Vermont, the summer days are short. The use of air conditioning is rare. We tend to rely on ceiling fans and window fans.

In the early morning, I open the blinds just a little bit. The windows are open so we can feel the fresh air. Then I close the sheer burgundy curtains to help block more of the heat from the sun. This helps keep the rooms cool and pleasant.

Housework and cooking are done in the early morning hours. If I work quickly, I can have most of my work done, and a load of laundry on the clothesline by 9 a.m. This leaves me plenty of free time to enjoy the *vacation - atmosphere* that summer tends to bring.

It is the most fun when all of us are home together. We often have company over most days. People tend to spend much more *leisure* time in the warm months than they do during the bitter winter season.

As strange as this may sound, I enjoy cleaning and organizing on hot summer mornings, more than any other time of year. This is probably because it is an excellent form of exercise, and brings great results in the form of a neat and tidy house. There is nothing like hanging clothes on the line on a warm summer day. Washing dishes throughout the day to make sure the family can enjoy bbq's, watermelon and ice cream makes me happy. I also love to see the fans blowing, and a bit of warm sunlight sneaking through the window, making my clean house look like a humble vacation spot.

One of the most relaxing things to do, after my morning work is finished, is to sit outside in the heat of the day, with a cool drink, and watch the children laugh and play.

When night falls, I do some last minute housework. The house is dim, the family is quiet, and we are all resting. We think about all the exciting things we've done during the day, and look forward to the next set of adventures.

Being home, as a permanent fixture as a housewife, has many benefits. I have so much freedom to manage this place and our finances in a way that we can all appreciate. Because, really, if you think about it, **being home all summer is a vacation for many people**. I am just grateful I can be home all year long.

When Mother Falls into a Dangerous Rut

The problem did not dawn on me until I stood in the kitchen last night trying not to cry. Then a dish slipped to the floor and broke. I looked up, the tears could no longer be held back. I saw 2 bottles of laundry detergent still sitting on the living room floor - the ones I never managed to put away after grocery shopping a few days before. I was *tired* and my nerves were frazzled.

Amy (16) saw the black streaks of mascara running down my cheeks. She sympathized. Then she got me settled in the other room and told me to rest. She found an old VCR tape of the *I Love Lucy Show* and told me to watch it. After two episodes I was no longer crying. I was happy again and well rested.

What was this rut I got into? I stopped exercising. . . I stopped taking breaks. . . Mr. White had several days off from work, but I was busy doing hours and hours of homeschooling, errands and housework each day. I did not rest. *I forgot.*

I remember cleaning and tidying the living room. I remember saying, "I'll just do this one last thing, then I really need to get some rest." But I continued working. Mr. White came over to me. . there was an intervention. . He put his hand on my arm and said,

"No. Stop. Go rest now." He was concerned. He sees that once I start cleaning, I cannot stop myself. . .

I must remember to rest. God provided us with work to do, but he also tells us to rest. Please don't ever let me forget. I don't want to be crying in the kitchen again with broken dishes at my feet.

For my own sake and well-being, I will cultivate the art of making a **mess** look *neat*.

A Quaint and Quiet Life at Home

Despite the fact that I am *surrounded* by teenagers; Despite the *noise* of their generation's music; Despite the occasional sibling *arguments* or the *rolling of the eyes* when it's time for chores, I am going to have a quiet life at home.

There needs to be solemn moments of meditation for my mood and demeanor to be prepared for this family. I need to rise while it is yet night to visit the prayer chamber. I need to look out the window at God's beautiful world . . . after several moments of taking in the Psalms or Proverbs from my treasured, vintage Bible.

When I wash the floors . . . do the dishes . . . vacuum . . . or do laundry, I am in my own little quiet world. I am grateful for these tasks, these labors that allow me some **solitude**. For where do you think the children go when there are chores to do? They invent homework or offer to clean their own rooms. They cheerfully run- off before they are asked to help me with *my* work. **This is my plan.** They have their own tasks and I **must** have *mine*. This is for my sanity.

Looking out the window as the sun begins to set, after a long day of work, I happily sigh. I see that there is more to my feeble soul than just pride in this day's accomplishments. I see the grandeur of God's amazing world in the landscape out my parlour window. I see the dark clouds coming and I see the beautiful trees and lovely front garden. It is a quaint and quiet life when one sets one's mind on eternal matters.

The Home Must be Occupied

In today's busy world, families are away from home more and more. Even stay-at-home Mothers are doing an enormous amount of traveling, doing errands, and going out on a daily basis. There is something missing at home.

There has to be a way to cut back on outside activities and *cultivate a home.* We need to spend more time on the home arts - cooking, baking, cleaning, hospitality. We need to make Home *the Base of our lives.* That base must have a strong foundation. We need to spend a lot of time there to keep it sturdy and secure.

I realize older children have jobs or events they attend. I understand they often need transportation. But something has to be changed in order for Mother to occupy the home.

There is a saying, "Keep the home fires burning." Someone had to be at home to keep the place warm. They kept up with the cleaning and baking and laundry. Someone was there on a regular basis and that someone was Mother.

I want to see my children come and go out in the world. I want them to look forward to coming home, finding me there, and telling me all about their adventures. I want to help nourish them and make them comfortable and warm and happy. **I need to be here** in order for that to happen.

Somehow, some way, *in order to have the old fashioned family survive*, Mother must **occupy** the home. To occupy is to reside. It is to be there. It is to keep busy on projects related to the home. Mother is the shining light of the family.

May her smiling presence at home be the greatest gift to the family.

Cleaning the Museum

As I worked through the house yesterday, I thought of my home as a museum. I found "vintage floors" with "exposed" wood underneath (on account of the torn linoleum). I found cracked door frames. I swept stairs which were in "old" condition. There were cobwebs in out-of-the way areas. I had to sort and archive files and bills and other such family histories.

I became the keeper of the Museum.   I was the mistress and secretary of this estate. It made things so much more fun!

We "take" guests here-and-there and do our best to make sure they are comfortable while they visit. We provide refreshments. We show them around the quaint rooms, with the mismatched furniture.

I spend much of the day taking care of this old place and the lovely people who reside here. I want their remembrances of home to be unique and endearing.

Torn carpets and other such nonsense are part of the charm of my home. Thus, it is when I am *cleaning* that I am most attached to this old place.

The Retired Life at Home

I spent much of the day reading near the fire. The children did their schoolwork at the table. I mused over the delightful writings of Dickens' "Dombey and Son."

Here and there, I commented about the story and entertained the children with quaint sayings and the brilliant use of words.

I shall describe my special parlour. There is a kitchen stool near my chair. This is typical for my reading time. I sip from a wine glass full of ginger-ale. I often have a china plate loaded with mini-marshmallows and chocolate chips.

A lovely wicker chair was given to me, *just yesterday*, by Nana. She had it sent up in the early evening. It is very comfortable.

We also have a set of antique chairs, which came with the purchase of our old 1800's house. They are stately and dignified chairs, if there ever was such a thing!

My book rests on a small footstool. This wooden marvel was

hand- made by Grandpa, many, many years ago- for my children when they were very young.   It is a family treasure.

Now, I must say, if you walked into my home and saw the humble furnishings, you might think we were living in poverty.

I don't agree.

A Serene and Quiet Life at Home

Everyday I walk outside and enjoy the cool winter air. I walk part of the property in silent contemplation. It is lovely to be at home. It is like a retired life to be a housewife.

Sure, there are trials and work and activity. But this is part of a normal life. The trick is, to somehow live in my own little world so that the stresses of the day do not destroy me.

Rising early is my secret weapon against pressure. The family sleeps, while I sit and read or write. I have hours in the dark morning, before the sun rises, to enjoy some solitude. Then I can clean and cook and bake and chat.

The phone rings all day long. There are dishes to do. There are floors to sweep and laundry to attend. I enjoy having duties which keep me occupied in the gentle arts of homemaking.

I pray here and there, throughout the day. I take long leisurely rests. I enjoy good books and hand-sewing projects. I think in elaborate ways - that my humble old house is an estate! This keeps me content and happy.

Sometimes, I listen to calming classical music while I work. I get all dressed up to keep house. I will even wear pearls. I don't do this every day, just when I need to cheer up and remain focused on lovely thoughts. My kitchen becomes another world. It is a delightful world! I bake cookies in my Edwardian Apron with my hair swept up. I listen to charming music and smile. I am at peace. I have to make those moments calm, with lots of effort, but they are worth it!

Home is the most delightful place on earth. May your day be filled with happy moments!

A Lovely Day for Cleaning

I had no plans for today and didn't know what I wanted to do. Can you imagine having a day off in the middle of the week?

The warmth of the morning and the beautiful sunshine streaming through my windows made me realize it would be lovely to clean!

I have been inspired lately by visiting a library in town. It is a historic building with amazing architectural detail. Large, stately, antique furniture is in every room. There are also paintings and drawings on the walls, which gives one a history lesson of the area. It is mesmerizing. *Hmmm...* Then I thought, *"I wonder if I can do something similar to my house?"* Well, my parlour already looks like that. But now to work on some of the other rooms!

My cleaning for today will be partially practical and partially creative. I shall make a long list of cleaning adventures - like vacuuming the staircase and polishing banisters. I will wash the sliding glass doors and throw out some clutter. But to make it even more exciting, I will note how long it took me to complete each item. This because I only want to work for the morning. I will only clean for 2 hours and then be free for the rest of the day.

This timed list will keep me motivated to work very fast, just for the challenge of it. I will also be able to refer to this list later when I have spare minutes and want to clean something.

*Perhaps a child will walk by and **beg** to do one of my chores from the list.* (gentle smiles) Because I make it look like such fun!

When I am finished, perhaps my home won't look exactly like that historic library, but it will be charming and lovely enough for me!

Spiritual Homemaking

I read somewhere that, long ago; a group of peasants would meet together for morning worship before they started their day's labor. The joy from that meeting filled their hearts and minds with holiness and it stayed with them while they worked. It has been reported that the sound of their hymn singing echoed through the fields. Then at the noon hour when they dined on their humble food, they eagerly sought the comforting words from the Bible and the warmth from their joint prayers. They were again able to go back to work with that same joy. In the evening, after the work was completed, their worship time refreshed them on their path in this life, and kept them going with pleasant thoughts of Heaven and doing God's work. They knew where the source of life came from.

Yesterday I read from the journal of John Wesley (1700's). He wrote how he spent his days, while on a ship with fellow laborers during a week's time. They rose at 4 am for private prayer, had public prayer and did all manner of religious duties throughout the day. The private prayer time included Bible reading, praying and learning. He also encouraged passengers and taught those, who were eager to learn, of God's way.

How can I not be ashamed when I compare my own life with those who have gone on before me?

I am caught up in the distractions of a modern world, and listening to the lies of a culture. It is a constant, daily battle to even attempt to do as Wesley and the Peasants did!

In our homemaking, we can find an efficient way to keep house and be good mothers while we spend our time in spiritual endeavors.

- We can listen to sermons (on the computer, CD or DVD) while we dust and sweep and wash.

- We can sing old time hymns (or listen to them) while we work.

- We can force ourselves (through discipline) to have daily Bible time twice each day (morning and evening, which is the least we can do, and was the custom of Christians for centuries.)

- We can choose to pass aside pop literature of today, or meaningless gossip-type biographies, and choose wholesome, old time books, which will encourage us on our holy way.

Remember that the *center* and *foundation* and *purpose* of our lives, is to glorify God and enjoy him forever (as the catechism says). This must be our focus, which will pour out with joy to those around us.

The result of this Spiritual Homemaking: A face that shines (like the veiled Moses on the mount) with radiant holy joy. How can that not impact and inspire those around us?

A Formal Dinner

The Dinner hour is one of the most happiest times for the family. They eagerly look forward to homemade cooking and spending time with everyone. Many linger over rolls and mashed potatoes while chatting.

Mother tidies up the dining room, or kitchen table, and makes it look pleasant. Children help set the table and start serving. Dinner preparations were often begun a few hours before the meal. Cleaning and cooking and baking were a pleasant process for the proud housewife. She wanted the evening meal to be a lovely family gathering.

It was common for every member of the family to have assigned seating. This was expected and familiar. Father was at the head of the table, and led the prayer.

The formal dinner at home, was where many learned their manners. They "passed the salt," or the butter, to the person beside them. Someone might get up to get that second platter of bread for the center of the table. But one of the nicest things about dinner is that it was formal. No one grabbed a plate to eat in front of the television. They wanted to be with the family and loved the special food.

Like many Mothers of today, I have been slacking in this area. I have forgotten how precious a *formal* dinner can be. I will start cooking and cleaning around 3 p.m. this afternoon. I will take my time and enjoy the process. I will not wear myself out all morning doing other things. There will be no rushing about at the last minute. There will be no quick trip to the grocery store for a forgotten item. I will be unhurried and peaceful. I will set the table and get out my serving bowls for a simple meal of baked ziti with bread and butter. We will have glasses of iced lemonade and have a precious time.

Right after dinner, I will rush out the door to take the children to youth group. But at least we will enjoy the leisure pace, of a lovely dinner time.

The Gentle Art of Home Keeping

A new day has started and it is a lovely time to start tending the home. We need to make sure we are awake early enough to start working in an unhurried, peaceful way.

There is often some kind of uniform to wear. This signifies our station in life. What makes you proud to be a housewife? Does it show in your clothes? In the way you style your hair? In your choice of jewelry? Getting dressed in something suitable for homemaking is a good start for the day. It's your choice if you want to make it classy, professional, or something more casual. I remember watching an old episode of *The Donna Reed Show*. The Mother was doing some heavy cleaning around the house. She had a kerchief in her hair and was wearing "trousers." Her daughter was appalled at how her mother looked and asked her not to wear those slacks if she went to the market. It would have embarrassed her to have her friends see her mother like that. Can you imagine how much times have changed?

Sometimes housewives would shop in the store with curlers in their hair. They were getting ready for an evening event, or a dinner party, but would be in public like that. In our area, I occasionally see someone in a "housecoat" (or bathrobe) while running in to buy a loaf of bread and a gallon of milk. It is sweet and nostalgic to see it because we know they are doing errands "for the home" and it is precious. But for the most part, we housewives will want to dress for the job, signifying to our children and those around us what we do.

There is so much to do in the home. We can have projects - like gardens (or even a small indoor flower pot); decorating, organizing, polishing and entertaining. Home is the center of our social life. It is here we interact with family and friends. Sometimes I think about a grand hotel lobby in all its elegance. We can have something like this, on a humbler scale in our parlour (or living room). Adding a few touches like a candle, decorative pillow, or some classical music can create a similar ambiance in the most sparsely furnished room.

We all have busy days and errands and such to keep us occupied. But perhaps we can slow it down a little. Instead of rushing through it all, for the sake of getting it done and over with, maybe we can enjoy each item on our to-do list. Maybe we can make it more fun by adding grace and beauty to our tasks.

Yesterday afternoon, I rushed through making a quick lunch because we had an appointment. I was flustered and harried. This is not the kind of thing I want to remember with joy. We have to fight against this each moment of our lives. There should be a gentleness to Mother's life. This is one of the reasons *Motherhood* is such a precious word. Each day, we must fight against taking on so much that it makes us abrasive. We need to have more patience, and this comes with daily practice, and accepting failure. Over time it will come, if we keep at it.

One of my favorite things to do is listen to one of four things while I am working around the home:

1. Old Time Gospel Music (Like Ralph Stanley or Roy Acuff).

2. Sermon on CD.

For The Love of Christian Homemaking

3. Classical Music.

4. The wind blowing and birds chirping out the window.

We can make home a very precious place, with our gentle actions and attitude. We renew our minds each morning with the motivation and excitement of the job of housewifery. It is an honored profession to be a keeper of the greatest place this side of Heaven - HOME!

Mother's Dinner Bell

Late yesterday afternoon, I rang the dinner bell for the first time of the season. I never ring the bell in the frigid winter months because the children are rarely outside. But now that the snow has melted and the warm sun has appeared, it is time to get back to my supper time tradition.

Years ago, when we bought this 1800's house, there was an auction conducted on the grounds by the previous owner. They had lived here so long and had accumulated many things. My husband and I bid on several items - including an old wooden wagon that sits on the front lawn. I also got this bell. I just had to have it.

Once we got settled in our new home, Grandpa (who, along with Nana, lives with us in an in-law apartment of the house) installed it on my front porch. I have had so much fun with it ever since.

When the children were little, I did training sessions. (smiles) They would be out playing in the back yard. I would grin and tell them to come running whenever they heard the bell. They thought it was such fun. Eventually, when I rang the bell, it meant that I needed them for something or that supper was ready. It sure saved me a lot of walking through the property to tell them what I needed!

Yet there is also a charming sense of nostalgia when Mother rings a dinner bell. It reminds me of my own childhood. My Great Aunt Rita lived across the street from us. She would ring the bell for her grandchildren to come running, just as she did for her own children when they were little. Our neighborhood had a beautiful private beach at the end of our street. This is where we children often played. There was a small playground, beach house, plenty of sand, and places to explore. Auntie Rita's house was up a hill, directly across from the beach. She would ring that dinner bell to call her children home.

Sometimes I would be out in my yard, and I would hear the ringing of the bell. I loved it. It comforted me. It made me so proud of Aunt Rita. I wanted to be like that, and have a home like that - where Mother called her children home, *each night*, for supper.

Today, my children are mostly grown. Two of my children have moved into their own homes. I only have three older teenagers left here at home. They have outgrown many of my *mother customs* - like bedtime stories. So yesterday, when I rang the dinner bell for the first time of the season, none of my teens came running. I smiled. . .

I headed out to the back property and had to remind them. "*Didn't anyone hear me ring the bell?*"

They grinned at me. "*Yeah, we heard you,*" said one of the mischievous ones.

[Mother] - "*When I ring the bell, you're supposed to come running. It means I need you or that supper is ready. . . But just now was only a **bell-drill**.*"

My older son perked up, "*Oh, did you make supper?*" I told him I was just about to. "*Well,*" he said in his gallant way, "*When supper is ready, ring it again and we will come running.*" I was delighted!

I love that the children humor my old ways. I love that even though they are "too old" for some of the Mother things I do, they still play along, in their own humorous way. And no matter what, I will still ring the dinner bell. Because someday, I will have grandchildren here, like at Auntie Rita's house. I will ring the bell for them . . . as a memorial of suppertime tradition. Those little ones, the next generation of children, will come running. . . *and they will love it*!

The Home Road to Heaven

Last night, as I cleaned the kitchen in the late hours of the day, I listened to a sermon on CD. It was a loud, old time preacher, and his words were encouraging and inspiring. The echo of his voice went throughout the rooms and we all heard as we worked.

One of my teens asked me a question about what the preacher was saying. I answered quickly and then was silent. We were all fairly silent as we went about our evening routine.

This morning, as I did my exercises, I listened to old southern, Classic Gospel Music, and it comforted me. This kind of "good propaganda" goes on in our home frequently, and it is necessary to keep us on a straight path despite a maze of choices in this life.

We read our Bibles, but not as often as we should. We sing hymns, but not like we should. Our daily failures only make us realize how very fragile we are, and how much we need the Lord each and every day.

This early morning, before my family wakes up, I am preparing my mood and my mind for the labor before me. It is more than just a mother's hospitality of cooking and serving. It is about ministering and encouraging them all toward heaven. For Home is my duty. But mostly, Home, *for us all*, is the road to Heaven.

Just for Company

Many of the old homes had china cabinets with dishes for special occasions. This helped make having company a lovely, exciting event! Mothers would have a nice clean room, freshly polished, for visiting. She would also welcome her guests into the kitchen for tea, coffee or some dessert.

When we are out on the road and weary from our travels, it is comforting to stop by to visit and have familiar things offered - like tea and cookies, near a warm fire. This strengthens us for the rest of our journey.

Ma and Pa Ingalls, in the 1800's, would buy white sugar when there was a little extra money. This was the *good* sugar and was saved *just for company*.

In some modern homes of today, there is a prevalent attitude of "**me**." The decor and the lifestyle reflect a selfishness, and a laid back casualness, that knows nothing of hospitality. Guests are told to wash their own cup and drink whatever is in the fridge. No tea or treats are handy, because that is not "*our way*," say the residents. "*People must accept us the way we are*," is their mantra. This sad state leaves weary souls *wandering* and seeking the refreshment of *home*.

When we set up our kitchens and living rooms in a way that *expects* to have company, there is a sense of joy and pride in doing good. We share our happy homes, even for a few hours, with dear friends and family. This helps cheer them on their way.

But most of all, when we have special things just for company, we tend to keep our homes cleaner. We tend to take care of our own appearance. We are ready for that knock on the door and are excited because we get to enjoy the special tea and cake that has been reserved for just such an occasion.

Yet, what of the children who beg to use the fine china, or have the special cakes *now*? Do we say we will use our company things for our own immediate family? Or will we smile with joy and say, "We will plan a special afternoon and invite company so we can use these things!" In this way, won't we teach them delayed gratification and how lovely it is to share our good things with others? Won't we teach them how special it is to scrub and polish the house, and work hard to prepare nice things, and get dressed up? Won't we teach them there is a difference, in life, from the daily routine, and special occasions? And that it isn't always just about *us*?

This is all something of an *ongoing* good deed. . . To share a few lovely things in life, in our homes, with those we care about. This brings out good manners in all involved. This brings a charm and a dignity to our characters.

Wouldn't it be lovely if we all had an annual Guest Book in the front hall, where visitors could sign, write the date, and leave a little note? Even if it was just our next door neighbor? What a lovely recording of the family history this treasure would be!

Housewife on Duty

A typical day for a housewife includes chores and "prettying" up the house. It is more fun when there is spring weather and birds are chirping. It makes one feel warm and cheerful.

In the morning, I clean the kitchen, then have tea. I do homeschool with my youngest, make treats, and do the little touches that create a home.

If I see an unmade bed, I make it. Whenever I walk into a room, I tidy it. It only takes a few minutes and brightens everyone's day.

In my childhood home, we always had clean dishes. If my mother saw a cup on the table, or in the living room, she would wash it right away. Things were kept up, *by cleaning as things happened.* It would have taken much longer to clean a piled up mess, than to clean here-and-there throughout the day.

My teenage daughter has not been feeling well. I made her a special lunch in the late afternoon. She sat on a stool and visited with me while I worked. I did a few dishes while I cooked. By the time we left the room, everything was back in order.

All this is having a housewife on duty. . . . Someone in charge of the management of the home. . . The Keeper. . . I am there if someone needs tea, or wants to know where the clean towels are. It is a delightful job that I am proud of. I am also greatly needed. What home doesn't need a housewife on duty? It is a blessing!

A very special reward came to me yesterday. My husband said he noticed the house had been extra clean lately and he appreciated it very much. He gave me some cash and said I could do whatever I wanted with it. I was shocked. But this made me realize something . . . - *he trusted me*. He trusted me with his home and he trusted me with his money. We live very *carefully and frugally*. For him to give me some extra money he had worked so hard to save, meant he knew I wouldn't waste it or be careless.

I had earned his respect and trust by my hard work and careful economies. But this is something I have to constantly strive for. We are *all* tempted to waste money or shop impulsively or be lazy. We must be on guard. This is also part of being a Keeper of the Home. We must watch out for *waste and sloth*.

There is a sense of pride when you are the Housewife on Duty. Each day we will improve in our skills. Each day is fresh and new. But for my husband to really trust me as his wife and the mother of his children and the keeper of his house? . . . This is one of the greatest of all accomplishments.

When Television Was Special

A Television set used to be a beloved piece of furniture. It was neatly dusted and polished. Some Mothers kept a white crocheted doily on the top, with a nice plant or some flowers. This was a lovely addition to the living room.

In the old days, families would gather around the radio to hear a nice evening program, *after the chores were finished.* There were a few programs that the children enjoyed, and others that the whole family wanted to hear. . . . In later years, this also happened with a TV set.

My Father worked hard at his job, and around the house. He had a large garage with a wood stove and a workshop. He was in charge of our garden and all maintenance for the cars and house. He also kept things tidy indoors, always cleaning up after himself. We children respected him and his need for rest. So when he wanted to watch a program, we children would sit on the floor, or couch, nearby and watch it with him. We saw many old westerns on Saturday afternoons.

On a weekly basis, we watched Lawrence Welk. We were always so excited when that program came on. We all enjoyed it so much!

We would have popcorn, or chips and just be together on those happy nights, watching television *with Mother and Dad.*

In those days, there was no such thing as a VCR or DVD player. We had never even heard of such a thing. If we missed a special movie . . .well. . .*that was that.* We could only hope it would come on again next year.

Most of our time was spent outside, or working, or at school. Television was special because most of the programs were wholesome and family centered. We would laugh and smile and be encouraged by genuine comedy in a time when vulgarity was unheard of.

I remember snowy winter nights, sitting by a roaring fireplace and watching Charlie Brown. This was a rare treat! We children would have already spent time in the kitchen, sitting together at the table, eating supper that Mother made. Then we would have our share of the chores, doing dishes, sweeping, and cleaning the table. When that work was finished, we could sit and enjoy a nice entertaining program and just relax and be happy.

Today, there are so many choices on television - almost too many. Sometimes I worry that television is such a magnet that *we could watch all our time away.* But the programs of this era can never compare to the sweet wholesome shows of yesteryear.

Mother's Stage

Daily life as a Mother is like a theatrical production. Mother is in the spotlight. She is the star of the show. Her stage is her home. She gets into character and portrays herself as the epitome of Motherhood.

She must focus on that performance. She must study the lines (duties and actions). She must focus on it and block most everything else out. She must be dedicated and give it her very best. How do I know this? Because William Holden and Bing Crosby were talking about it in *Country Girl.* (smiles) Bing portrayed a fabulous performer who had a difficult personal life. He gave everything he had when on stage, but stumbled and suffered between shows.

William Holden yelled at him and advised him. He also said something like this:

"Everyone has trouble at home. *Those who say they don't are lying. The ones who pretend they don't are the ones who have the most trouble."*

Does this sound like real life to you?

No successful actor can get on stage and do a half-hearted job. He must give it all he has. He must do his very best. His duties come first. He cannot let personal problems or trials get in the way of his work. *He can't give up.*

To be a *Mother Actress,* means we do our work, no matter what. We are performing on stage every single day. Can we have breaks? Certainly. Can we delegate from the couch when we are sick? Of course! But we must write those into our lines. Because in every moment of our lives, we have little ears listening and little eyes watching. We have *understudies* focusing on our every move, so they learn to imitate us in later life.

Does this mean Mother can't be mad, sad or grumpy? She most certainly can. She just has to incorporate them brilliantly into her lines. Her performances must be something to remember. She must do them in a way that is human, but in a way that is admirable. This takes practice. She will also learn from her failures.

When the spotlight shines on Mother, let her be as sweet as Doris Day and as dedicated as Grace Kelly and as dramatic as Bette Davis. May she analyze her performance and make it better at every show (each new day)! Home, *as Mother's Stage,* will be the greatest accomplishment of her life.

The Outside World

Sometimes, it is nice just to focus on the quiet life at home. But even more, it is good when there is no computer or television or even a radio. It is peaceful and silent. This is where we can get a little break from the outside world. We can be refreshed and just focus on reading, baking or puttering around the house.

I've had sort of a whirlwind of activities the last several days. Late one night some of my teens went to Youth Group at church, then we had guests over for The Passover meal. We were laughing and up late into the night. I managed to clean everything, and was so content to look around the neat rooms after such a busy time! I was also very proud of us all for doing such important things, despite all the extra work it creates!

On another day some of us drove into the city on a long journey. It was an all-day adventure. Most of the trip was uncomfortable and tiring, but there were so many rewards and wonderful things despite the negatives. (Just like life, I suppose.) We came home very late, but delighted to be home again, with good memories!

Next, it was church and that was just lovely! We sang some precious hymns and heard a good sermon.

Now I am trying to settle back into a quiet routine of being home and making a home. I have been listening to the *hum* of our wood pellet stove, pruning my indoor flower plants, and watching the rain through the window. Soon, I will start knitting and listen to sermons on CD and focus on eternal things. I will enjoy the retreat of home and, *just for a time*, ignore the outside world.

Mother's Cleaning Recovery

There are mood swings that affect the attitude; and then there are mood swings that affect a housewife's ability to clean.

Most of the time I want to clean, with an artist's creative heart. Other times, I clean for part of the day and am content. But sometimes, there is a mood of "recovery" that comes over me. This is when life has been overly busy or there have been too many events in a short amount of time and I get *mood weary* of housework. This is a special time, because I am weary, but not sick. I am good humored. I tend to make a lot of jokes with my family about my apparent lack of work.

One of my teens was doing a list of chores today. I then reminded him to make dinner. (smiles) He said, good naturedly, "I'm doing all *your* work now!" I told him, in my sweetest voice, "We *all* have to work around here." I then paused and said quietly. . . "*Except me*." He laughed. He knows I am in "recovery mode."

Earlier, we were in the car on an errand. We talked about how important hard work is and how we must all earn money for the things we want. I said those words again. . . "*Except me*." The children know I have a contract. * But we make jokes about it.

They know I work hard in the home. They also know I am in "recovery mode," which means I get all dressed up to do "nothing."

When I am recovering from cleaning or too much activity, I am peaceful and quiet and smiling a lot. I read and watch television. I do a little housework - just enough - and delegate the rest.

This is the sweetest time for me. I pace myself and enjoy home and life. But I know the most exciting part will come very soon - in a day or two - when all my energy has returned, and I am able to clean and work hard again. This, of course, is my favorite thing of all - taking pride in a lovely, well-kept home. I can't wait!

*Contract – This is a "housewife contract" my husband and I agreed to before we got married. He promised to provide for me and I would be the housewife. I would never have to work.

When Mother is Late for Her Shift

One morning last week, I overslept. I was "out" so long I missed my shift. This is the normal time that I start my housework. Of course, we had surprise visitors throughout the day. I tried to tidy the mess, but I had gotten so behind that it was difficult to be proud of my home.

I realize things get messy because we live here, and we need to cook and bake and do laundry. But if I stay on top of it all, it normally stays fairly neat. *This was not the case last week.* It would have been far better if I had only fallen asleep on the job.

How many of us have forced ourselves out of bed in the morning with a promise that we will get a nap later? Or how much we can't wait until night when we can sleep again? (smiles) Sometimes this is because of the cold weather. I can't imagine ever feeling that way on a warm summer day, or a pleasant spring morning. It must certainly have to do with the cold. But the brave mother, who starts the fire, (or has her husband do it, as in my incompétent case), will have a lovely, cozy start to her day.

It is the struggle against duty that must be overcome. We must remember that we can have breaks, and rests and times of leisure. These should be sacred to the soul, to keep our spirits up, and keep us going joyfully and peacefully.

This is why I love to keep my parlour clean and pretty. It is a pleasant place to sit and rest. It is also a beautiful place to greet visitors. Even if we only have one room decent and nice, most of the time, we can have a sense of accomplishment. We can gain strength in that room, to make the rest of the place look lovely.

Well, I am late again today, but not as late as last week. I will have to get some work done this morning, before the family rises. It is still quiet here. Mr. White has just started the fire in the parlour. I will make tea so I can calmly survey the damage this messy house has endured overnight (I have teenagers and was ill yesterday). But I will set it all to "rights" this morning. That will boost my spirits and also bring happiness to the family.

The Morning Duties

It is raining and cool at our Vermont Estate. The stove is out and the air is crisp. Soon Mr. White will start the fire and another day will begin. I have a kitchen to clean, a floor to mop, laundry to wash, and food to cook. I will also bake brownies this morning.

I shall have tea while I read my Bible and do my Prentiss Study. I will enjoy the silence while everyone still sleeps. It is a quiet time of preparation for the morning duties.

Perhaps I will go out and do a little visiting this afternoon. I will bring some brownies with me, to share.

I also want to buy a new set of Knitting needles. On a cool, foggy day like this, I like to think about a Jane Austen Estate in England. It makes me want to sit by the window and do some hand-work, while contemplating lovely thoughts.

If I had little babies around, they would delight me with their antics and wear me out with their precious energy. But I would love it! Since my children are mostly grown, I long for the sound of little feet and giggling! This large old house echoes its emptiness and almost orders children to reside here. Someday soon I will have grandchildren to fill these halls and floors.

But for today, I will clean and cook and bake, like always. I will remember when my children were young while I wash dishes. I will smile as I think of the silly things they did and said while I wash the floors. And I will pray a silent prayer of thanksgiving for the memory and the present of a mother's life at home.

The Humble Home

I've seen so many lovely homes, beautifully decorated. . . I see families with money for gifts, nice clothes and expensive food. More and more families are expecting larger homes with more conveniences. They want more than one bathroom, double sinks, and plenty of small appliances to do all the hard labor in the kitchen. Many homes today have dishwashers, bread machines and food processors. But none of these items were in Grandmother's home. None of these items were in my childhood home. None of these items are in my current home.

There can be simplicity and joy in a humble home. Families with very little can still have a nice life. They can have happy homes, with a small purse and few possessions.

Inside their basic dwelling should be diligence, hard work, love, and service. . .

Sometimes I wonder if the humblest of homes, *with loving hearts of **great faith in God**,* are the sweetest homes of all.

A Lovely Home Life

I was in the city, shopping and travelling all day yesterday, with my three daughters. My oldest two live far away from me, and I rarely get to see them. But we carry "home" with us wherever we go. There is a dignity and an honor we have for our family name. We have certain habits, cultured conversations, mannerisms and humor that are with us to remind us of *Home* wherever we are. . . As long as we are together in heart and mind, in person, in a letter or on the phone, the loveliness of home will always be with us.

I love to visit the homes of my grown children. I love to see the decorations, the housekeeping and the foods they make. Their homes are an extension of mine. Their lives are an extension of mine. I am *grateful* to be their mother.

To add some culture to our homes, keeping it lovely, we try to avoid conflict. We try to make light of difficult situations. This limits the stressful moments. Instead, we bring in lovely things. This might be classical music or classic literature.

This can also mean classical conversation. . . The other morning I *commenced* the reading of *"Dombey and Son"* by

Dickens. This puts me in a distinguished kind of mood that **startles** and **amuses** my children.

Here are some examples:

I might say, *"You are to dine with the Smith family at the noon hour."* This translates as, "Your friend Joe Smith and his Mom are going to McDonald's and want you to go with them at 12:00."

Or, if one of the kids brings in the mail and says, "Oh, here is that letter you have been waiting for!"

I would translate this, in casual conversation, as *"The letter was announced."*

Listening to *Beethoven* while cleaning the kitchen, or serving homemade pizza on fine china, are special ways of making home lovely.

Painting my old kitchen an elegant sage green and calling my purple living room a Parlour are other ways to make things lovely.

These little daily actions of creating beauty and happiness are examples of loveliness.

These little touches of *grace* and refinement make even the most humble home a happy place to be. My grown children have often said to me, *"Mom, we never knew we were poor. You always acted like we were rich."*

Spoiling Breakfast

I have to admit this. . . I would rather eat cookies and chips than a real breakfast. I will even make a nourishing breakfast for my children, but take **none** for myself.

The problem is that I have little self - control when it comes to snacking. If I even eat one brownie, I am too full for a real meal. It's called "spoiling your dinner," even if it was only breakfast.

I have no problem creating a lovely ambiance for the evening meal. I have no trouble with the time involved in setting the table, lighting candles, and making a delicious, yet humble, dinner.

But in the morning, I have trouble taking all that time to enjoy a nice breakfast. On the days I actually sit down at the table with tea, toast and a little fruit, I feel like I have accomplished a lot!

Most mornings, I do a tremendous amount of housework before the family even wakes up. I like to get most of my work out of the way. Breakfast, for me, would be like taking a break.

Do you remember the stories of farmers who would do morning chores before they even got to eat? It is also convenient to get moving, and work hard before enjoying a nice meal.

There were times we had grits, cantaloupe, eggs and biscuits for a pleasant, southern style breakfast. Other days we would have fresh baked muffins and fruit. Plain cereal is healthy and quick, but not very exciting. Pancakes are too filling and make me tired. (smiles) I have never liked eating eggs, but love making omelets for my children. A nice formal breakfast, after an early morning of chores, is a lovely way to start the day.

Perhaps dressing up for breakfast, using fine china, linen napkins, and a delicate tea pot would help make breakfast time a more formal, inviting affair. Even if I drink hot chocolate and have grits and toast, after doing some heavy housework, I would be more inclined to ignore the brownies so I can actually enjoy the breakfast hour.

As Sorrowful Yet Always Rejoicing at Home

Home is steadfast and secure. It can be anywhere your family is, in any city, in any country. And with that "home" comes trouble. There is heavy labor, and financial woes. There are aches of the heart and of the body. . . These are the sorrows that never seem to go away. But the joy of the family is **home**.

Many of us are busy with spring cleaning. It is overwhelming because it is extra work, in addition to our daily routine. There are clothes to sort and discard. There are closets to empty and clean. There are window sills to vacuum and wash. And perhaps a few rooms need a fresh coat of paint. It can be a heavy burden if we don't plan for it, or have enough cheerful helpers to make it a fun adventure.

Yet some of our normal routines are also exhausting and difficult. Hanging laundry on the clothesline or on the backs of kitchen chairs (on cold, rainy days) can wear us out. We spend hours in housekeeping, cooking and hospitality. Hopefully we love our work, but sometimes there are tears along with smiles. *This is the reality of life.*

There are no ordinary days; Even when they all seem like a blur of the same.

Dreams for better days and visions of happy events will always be in our hearts. This keeps us joyful.

We find peace and comfort in the monotony of our chores. We liven them up with the personalities and efforts of our creativity, and of our willingness to bring happiness to those around us.

Every time we wash dishes, or sweep the porch, we take one baby step closer to our heavenly reward. This brings us the greatest sense of accomplishment and a soaring joy that few can understand.

We Mothers need to be here - for the good times and the bad. We need to be the foundation of the family; the one that holds it all together, creating a warm, cheerful light in spite of a dark society.

"As sorrowful, yet alway rejoicing; as poor, yet making many rich; as having nothing, and yet possessing all things." - II Corinthians 6:10

When Mother is the Maid

It can be a status-symbol to have a housekeeper clean your house for you. I also read a great book by a Home Schooling Mother. She hired a live-in maid to take care of things. Obviously she had the extra money for that, and I love that she had domestic help. For most of us, however, hiring help is not in the budget.

Too many people today spend their time "chilling" or "hanging out." It is certainly fine to rest and take breaks, but more and more people are becoming lazy.

Cleaning our own homes includes *plenty* of daily work. In the 1800's, farm wives had plenty to do at home. They made meals, did dishes, tended gardens, preserved produce, made clothes, and cared for the entire family. In the 1930's it was common to spring clean the entire house by emptying the contents, scrubbing out cabinets and closets, and even painting all the rooms. There was an attitude of *work* more than *leisure* in those days.

There is a way to efficiently clean so that it takes less time. There is a way to delegate certain duties to different members of the family so the burden doesn't rest on one person. But Mother is the head housekeeper. She is the executive maid in charge of the entire home.

She must be careful not to take on too many outside projects or responsibilities. Her work at home, caring for the family and home, is substantial! It is *immense*. It is one of the greatest jobs in the world.

When Mother can be her own maid, with class and style, she is setting a fashion statement for the culture around her - *that staying home is something to crave* - something of value, that girls should want to aspire to. When she does her job cheerfully and with pride, she sets the stage for a role many others will want.

Family Comfort in the Evening Hours

At the end of the day, the family gathers together for a meal and to share adventures. Sometimes the children will laugh and entertain the others. Or, there will be older teens who talk about their work day.

In old time humble homes, everyone would gather around a vintage radio and listen to the news or a program. Mother would knit or do some mending. Father might be smoking a pipe or doing a little whittling. The children might have jacks to play on the floor, or a few handmade toys.

In other homes, someone would play the piano and all would gather round to sing. Or perhaps one could hear the sound of a banjo as the family sits on the porch playing some old country music and singing along.

In later years, with the invention of record players, the family could hear crooners like Frank Sinatra, and Bing Crosby.

Next, there were television sets where programs like *Burns and Allen* were broadcast. Families would eat their dinner at the table and then settle down to enjoy a show together.

Families play board games, cards and checkers. This is a wonderful form of togetherness which calms and soothes the hearts of weary souls.

In these days, we have modern radios with Christian stations for sermons, music, talk and advertisements. These are also heard on car radios as we travel on errands or trips. We also have CD players to hear modern music that we enjoy.

Some kind of entertainment goes on each night in most homes. This *comforts* and *cheers* the family at the end of a long, hard day.

It is something we can strive to create - an atmosphere of happiness, and entertainment with our families.

We should look forward to the setting of the sun, as we toil on with our work, as the best part of the day - the *night time* for rest and reward for our daytime labors.

Isn't this just like our *earthly life* as the daytime, and *eternal life* (at death) - as our night-time?

A Homemaking Lesson

[Learned from Mother White]

I learned to knit and crochet, as a young girl. One of my Aunts taught me some basic stitches. I continued to work with yarn on my own, until I was in my mid-teen years. . . By then I was too busy to bother with it anymore.

Somehow, I forgot how to do it. . .

I remember when I was pregnant with my first child. I was living with my husband's parents for a short time. I spent each day, at home, with Mother White (my husband's mother). She was the classic housewife and kept a lovely home. We would sit in the livingroom every afternoon and crochet while watching her soap operas.

I remember her re-teaching me how to work with the yarn. She would teach me a few stitches and then head into the kitchen to greet one of her visitors, or start cooking. I remember, repeatedly going back to her and saying, "*What was I supposed to do?*" or "*How do I do that stitch again?*" She patiently showed me, with a kind smile, and was proud of my efforts.

I never saw Mother White with a pattern, or book of stitches. She knew them in her mind, just like she knew her recipes. Because of the stitches she taught me, I still remember exactly how to crochet her way. To this very day, I can crochet a baby bonnet, blanket, or scarf from memory without having to think about it. The pattern is permanently embedded in my mind, where Mother White carefully, and patiently, passed it on to me - just like a valuable family recipe.

Rural Housewives

It is bitterly cold here in Vermont. We end up almost trapped at home. It's too cold to go outdoors, but we *must* for chores and errands. Winter is the time to settle inside near the fire, but it can be a very lonely experience.

One way rural housewives, in the old days, would pass the time was by listening to radio programs while knitting or sewing. This was during breaks from their household tasks. I have heard about something called, "neighboring over the air," or "radio housewives," which included programs of homemakers telling stories or sharing recipes over the airwaves.

There were other programs, including news segments, or ongoing stories that even the children would gather around to hear. These might be suspense, mystery or westerns.

I love the idea of sitting by a large piece of beautiful furniture that was called a radio, while mending or knitting. It would be a lovely way to pass the time.

Housewives would also do their baking and try to have something special in case an unexpected visitor came by. -*We need to keep the cookie jar and breadbox filled!*- When someone stops by our house, I love to have freshly baked cookies, brownies or fudge to offer our guests.

I realize rural housewives often feel alone. Sometimes they need a little encouragement, a funny story to cheer them up, or some little bit of advice about the work they do all day long. The radio programs and occasional neighborly visits were a blessing. Church services and other events were also greatly appreciated.

Today, radio programs are mostly talk shows, music or a myriad of commercials. Occasionally, we can hear something like *Adventures in Odyssey* while driving down the road, or listening in on the old kitchen radio. I wonder what would happen if they brought back a homemaking program on the radio? A little visit over the airwaves might be just what we need!

Fighting the Hectic Life

Home is to be a place of rest. The family should feel at ease and secure. If they are stressed from activities and the pressure of deadlines, or too many projects, there will be tension and misery.

A grumpy husband is soothed by a pleasant environment and a calm wife. Rambunctious children settle down when they become familiar with a structured routine.

A wife who doesn't take on too many projects, can tend to her home and family duties with a sweet demeanor.

Often, we mothers put too much pressure on ourselves to accomplish too much, and it only leaves us weary.

We certainly have a list of daily tasks, but if they are a regular habit - a routine, we can handle them with an unhurried approach.

We make home a precious place, when we tend to our work in a sweet and steady manner.

Daily we must fight the mentality of being overly busy. We must deal with the onslaught of potential clutter of both *things* and *life*, so our homes can be places of peace and rest.

The sweetest reminder of having a peaceful life is to take care of a newborn baby. A baby brings out the quietest, most patient devotion in a mother. This helpless, precious infant makes everything else seem meaningless, as Mother sits in a rocking chair *for hours*, humming lullabies and cuddling that small child.

When the baby is content, mother tidies the house and smiles to the family. She looks over the crib, of that sleeping baby, with the greatest sense of joy. She has won the battle of giving up the hectic life, and traded it for a peaceful, *settled* life at home.

Pleasant Hours at Home

I love to see everyone happy and busy at home. There should be plenty of projects available so that boredom does not creep in. We have cards, board games, sewing projects, Drawing materials and such, to occupy ourselves during our leisure hours.

In the winter time, it is good to have sleds, shovels, and other fun tools to keep children busy. The children will run in and out of the house, with exciting news, or to take a hot chocolate break.

Summer time is the most fun - with pools, bikes, toys and picnics to entertain the family for many hours in the fresh air.

As a Mother, I enjoy preparing foods, cleaning, tidying, and making things look nice. But I love to do this when everyone around me is happy and chatty.

As a Wife, I love to see my husband resting or watching television while I am busy working on the home arts.

When we have the older children home for a visit, or guests stop by, I want them to have plenty to do - like playing pool in our game room, or watching a nice movie.

Home is a place of industry and rest. . . *And Mother is the* **hostess** *of it all.*

A Paper Plate Society

Years ago, in home economics class, we students learned how to set a pleasant table. We were told that dining together as a family was an experience. We felt that it was an essential part of family values. The table didn't have to be fancy, but the basic elements were there:

Plates, silverware, a napkin at each place, cups, and serving bowls in the center.

I've noticed that families are using paper plates on a regular basis.

Here is the problem:

- They tend to make people eat more. Why? Because we eat quickly. Paper plates are for fast and easy meals.

When we sit together and dine at the table, the meal goes slower. We visit with one another, smile and enjoy the food. We tend to eat less. The experience is savored and enjoyed.

Our society loves paper plates because *no one wants to clean.* The plates are a modern substitute, creating a fast food environment. Something is wrong when we are too busy to sit down together as a family to enjoy the blessing of food.

Are paper plates wrong? *Certainly not.* But they should be reserved for emergencies, when someone is ill, occasional dining, or for picnics. Paper plates should be the rare exception, not the common rule.

What if you have a busy schedule and cannot find time to sit together? *Does that mean you have to use paper plates*? (gentle smiles) How about setting the table, whether for breakfast, lunch or dinner, with real dishes and enjoying the meal with whoever happens to be there. Meal times are commonly at specific times and should be an expected routine. This helps keep order and security in the home.

Dine alone, at times, if you must, but please use real plates. (gentle smiles)

The Blessing of Being a Half-Southern Mama

My father is from rural Alabama and my mother is from suburban Massachusetts. We grew up in a beautiful, wealthy town, south of Boston. But the culture of my father's life was with us every moment. We travelled to Alabama many times. My Uncle was a minister and had a small church; packed with the sweetest people you could ever meet. Many cried with joy, or repentance, at his revival meetings.

Have you ever heard the beautiful, humble songs of the saints in those old rural churches, down south? The melody echoes in my memory, even after all these years. The thought of them brings tears to my eyes.

When poor, gospel country clashes with rich, majestic values, there is a shaking of the character. There is a yearning for a life that is true and poor (in worldly goods) and grateful.

There is a reason this old reserved New Englander has a tremendous attachment to the old southern ways. I live in a cold society. It is full of culture and worldliness. But my heart is in the memories of the old Alabama life.

It is the world where Grandma wore pretty dresses, and spoke with such a deep accent, I could never understand her. She had the sweetest heart! I can still see her smiling, walking across the hill on the family property.

I remember her old house. It was humble and precious and just like something you would see in a movie from the 1930's. It was a white, 2 story, with a large covered front porch. The furniture was clean and neat and simple. Mothers in those days would set out tablecloths and bring you a drink with lots of ice. They would make sure you were happy! The home and the neighborhood were nothing like the suburban area in which I lived. It seemed like rural Alabama homes held the hardest working, strong families you could ever meet.

I remember living there for part of a summer, as a teen, and being given some lovely dresses. They fit me perfectly and were homemade. I only wish I still had them. You can't find beautifully made fashion like that anymore.

The Bible was the book everyone wanted to read. It sat predominately where all could see it. It was treated with the greatest respect.

I cannot even remember anyone not going to church. Everyone got dressed up and went together. Oh, and the music of that time is outstanding. Famous gospel singers openly loved the Lord. You could hear it in their songs. They knew where the real money came from - singing the old godly songs, knowing the reward was in Heaven.

The homes were neatly kept and lovingly cared for. The summer heat was intense but just right. There were gardens and delicious home-cooking. Neighbors watched out for neighbors and were friendly and thoughtful.

The sermons in the old country churches would melt the heart of the coldest sinner. They touched the soul and would never leave you. This is the southern culture that has stayed with me all these years. And so I listen to old gospel songs, from the likes of

Roy Acuff and J.D. Sumner to help me stay strong in this cold-hearted world around me.

Sometimes I wonder what will become of my children, who have never been down south. But I know that my habits and values from those memories are vivid in their daily lives. Somehow, they may just become half-southern without even realizing how it happened.

The reality of what I crave from this heritage is old American values frozen in time. That is what the southern lesson is to me. It is the memory of what *was*, and what I must keep alive each and every day of my life.

A Home with Character

I love strolling through old neighborhoods and seeing the lovely old houses. My favorite place to walk is on Main Street in Hingham, Massachusetts. The houses are hundreds of years old. They are large and elaborate and amazing!

I love seeing wrought iron gates, stately trees and towering windows. I wonder if the people inside are having tea time in the drawing room? Or are they sitting together near the fire, while one of them reads aloud from *"Great Expectations"*?

Every day, I strive to make my house look like it has character. But it needs a "keeper" to do all the work. Sometimes I have trouble organizing my time enough to do those little things that bring out the best in this old estate.

So today, I will do a little extra work around here. It will be a work of love - *the love of character*. Then perhaps, *when twilight comes*, I will sit near the fire and read from Dickens.

Make the Mess Look Pretty

What happens when Mother is too weak, or worn out, to clean? Lately, my main pastime is making the messes look neat.

I walk into the kitchen, see all the work I have to do, and instead of cleaning it, I tidy it up. I wipe down counters, stack dishes and just make it all look pretty.

It's not that I don't *want* to clean. I enjoy my work, especially when I listen to sermons or old time gospel on my kitchen radio. But I am so wiped out, physically, that I can barely function.

However, I think I can manage some work this morning. I should just do my marathon cleaning. I will have to give myself a full hour, rather than the standard 30 minutes. I need the extra time, to drag myself though the chores. (smiles)

I should probably include the children in this. . . Maybe I will write them chore letters? Or perhaps I will hand out chore cards?

I think the cards would be better, since letters would take more work for me.

After the hour is up, hopefully I will have cleaned the parlour, washed sheets, done laundry, cleaned the kitchen, and vacuumed. If that timer goes off, and I am not finished, I will just organize the mess, tidy it up and make it all look lovely.

Then I will happily rest for the day!

Mother's Rose – Colored Glasses

Imagine walking through life seeing all things, hearing all things and being constantly bombarded with reality - emotions, drama and stress. This is not an easy kind of life. Now imagine, instead, a delicate pair of rose - colored glasses. Once a Mother puts these on, she cannot hear as well. Her vision is a little blurred, and her focus is not entirely clear. Her sharp focus is weakened and this relieves a great deal of pressure on her delicate soul.

She can walk through life in a subdued world, where she is more sheltered and protected from the unloveliness of real life. When she wears these glasses, she becomes more gentle, more meek and more kind. Why? Because she becomes just a little bit handicapped and fragile, and this will greatly affect her demeanor.

The Charm of the Old Days

Looking at pictures of American society from previous generations makes me nostalgic for the old days. These can be any days from the past that are precious, or charming, or pleasant.

Do you remember when people would get all dressed up to go to the store? Or when a visitor would come by the house, and the hostess was already dressed nicely? Girls would get their sweater and take a nice leisurely walk to visit with their guest. They were un-hurried and enjoyed the fresh air without the distractions of modern technology that we, of this generation, have so much trouble trying to control.

These old- day- pictures make me want to find some sewing patterns and make my own pretty clothes. These are classic items one cannot find in the stores anymore.

I also want to get a soda from the soda fountain! Or take a walk through the center of town, stopping at the library for a bit, or getting an ice cream with a friend.

The *patience* of the old days is astounding. There was not the constant rush to do it all. Moms were generally at home and available for any crisis that came up. These mothers were not overtaxed with too many commitments, or too many projects. They were the slow-paced, enjoy- the- daily- life kind of Mothers who had the energy and will to help when the need arose.

Children who came home to such a place, where Mother was relaxed and happy, were the luckiest children on earth.

I wonder if we can take a little of yesteryear's charm and create some modern nostalgia for the next generation?

Designed to Comfort Us

Sometimes when I drive my teenagers on an errand, we stop at a little store at the corner of an intersection. Across the street is a large church. We can hear a gentle sound of hymns being played from the church bells. It is lovely. The sound calms my nerves. It soothes me. It takes my mind to heavenly things, and off my daily troubles. I am grateful to them. I wonder if they know it is a blessing to those walking by?

Sometimes I leave my Bible on the kitchen table, or the hutch counter. When I am busy doing chores, I absentmindedly notice it and touch the cover. It slows me down for a moment, and turns my thoughts off this difficult life.

The Church, The Bible, Prayers, and Religious Duties are all designed to comfort us. They are there so we can take a break from the constant, stressful demands in this life. How would we ever survive without them? Wouldn't the light and the salt be removed? How, then, can we ever consider the neglect of these essential duties?

The Danger of Being an Unproductive Housewife

There is a danger in having nothing to do. Many housewives get bored at times, when they don't have a sort of vision. They need to be creative, inventive and productive.

Recently I read a post describing a barrenness in life. This is an emptiness. It made me think of a withered fruit tree that is unprofitable. This kind of barrenness can cause intense depression, misery and sadness. (It can also be caused by doing **far too much** that we are no longer producing good. This, too, is unproductive.)

We all know that when our children are idle, they get into trouble. But with Mothers, if we don't have something to do, we spiral into sadness. A dark cloud comes over one's life.

When the housewife is sick or incapable of doing anything, she may read or have visitors while she is recovering. She is still being productive while she heals. But the housewife who is perfectly well, needs to find things to do that **she enjoys**, or that *creates* something.

The Lord said, "Occupy until I come." Did that mean to keep busy? To keep producing?

What about, "Do **all** to the glory of God?"

And certainly we are commanded to rest one day of the week, and also to rest at night. It is a special, deserved rest that feels rewarding after accomplishing much, in our own small way, for the Lord.

I wonder if being productive - whether in prayer, Bible studies, visiting others, creating, baking, caring for babies and children, or what have you, we are creating a fruitfulness in our lives that will bless us, and those around us.

Yet there is another danger - it is far more serious. It is the danger of doing too much. It is a danger of taking on the whole world and destroying a restful spirit. It can make one angry, physically ill, and depressed.

In other cultures, such as Italy, family is the center of life. The people work, but at a slower pace. I also read a lovely passage from *"Stepping Heavenward."* The main character, Katy, was so overburdened with household tasks that she was ill and irritated. Her husband soothed her, advising her to take on only the work she was capable of. He said something like, *"once you feel yourself getting upset, or burdened, stop at once to rest, and be refreshed."*

We are to be productive, but the ideal way for that is to do it at a steady, calm pace. This is a *mysterious* sort of way. It is keeping busy in an almost romantic way. It is determined, but tender. It is cheerful and pleasant, and produces lovely things in the heart and life.

The Comfort of Tea Time

My favorite memory of home is of having tea. It is comforting to serve tea to guests, to visit with family over tea, and to watch sweet little girls enjoy playing with tea sets.

When we are blessed with pretty china cups, we feel rich. There is something soothing and relaxing about sitting down to a neatly decorated table and being served hot tea in a pretty cup. It is even sweeter to drink tea while visiting and eating a few delicate cookies.

Have you ever tried *Lorna Doones?* I was introduced to them two decades ago, while in the hospital, after the birth of one of my children. Late at night, a nurse brought me a few of these delicious cookies. I loved them! To this day, eating Lorna Doones still bring me a nostalgic smile. They are a rare treat. I love to have them with my tea.

A few years ago, I was in a Cracker Barrel restaurant in New Hampshire. They served English tea with my breakfast. To me, it was just like being at home. I felt comfortable and happy. I wonder if hot tea is a New England tradition? Because when I was a teenager, I traveled to Alabama. We went to a restaurant and when I ordered tea, they served me a tall glass of iced tea. I did not understand. (smiles) I had thought everyone in the world drank hot tea in pretty china cups.

The Kitchen is Ready

I usually clean my kitchen three times a day. This includes wiping down appliances, counters, sweeping and cleaning the sink.

There is nothing worse, when it comes to housekeeping, for the family to wonder why there are no clean dishes. It is a black mark on my record, and makes me look like a slacker in the eyes of my family. Sure, we all have our own chores, but the kitchen is mostly my domain. I am expected to run a clean place because that is my job.

Have you ever heard the joke that when Mom cleans the kitchen, she tells the family they have to eat out because she doesn't want it to get messed up again? (smiles) But there is a better mind-set. Once the kitchen is clean, how about stepping back with pride and saying to the family:

"The Kitchen is Ready."

In other words, it has been cleaned. It is ready for guests. It is ready for anyone who wants to cook or have something good to eat. It is all set!

In this house, no one can clean like Mother. This is evidenced when I am ill and bedridden. Right now, I only have one helper left at home. And he willingly takes over my chores. I often hear his eager voice say, "*I'll do all the dishes for you, Mom. You just rest!*" And then a few hours later, the same child says, "*I did some of the work. Can I do the rest tomorrow?*" I just smile...

24 hours later, not only is the kitchen a disaster, but so is the rest of the house. Honestly, I have a hard time cleaning that kind of mess and think it would have been easier to just clean through my illness! (smiles)

But the children really appreciate a hard working mother. They miss hearing me say:

"Hey, you guys... The kitchen is ready!"

They come running from all over the place. They want to cook in a clean kitchen. They make snacks, get drinks and smile with delight.

They always know when Mother is home and well, - *Because the kitchen is clean.*

Homemaking Links the Generations

As I work around the house today, I am thinking of my childhood. We had an old radio in the living room. It was a large piece of furniture and had a "72" record player inside. My Father also had an 8 - track player we kept on a bookcase near the lamp.

I remember the sweet sounds of old time music. It made me think of hard working families who loved home and cared about the basics of daily life, rather than materialism.

Today, I am cleaning and listening to Pandora Radio on a gospel music station. I hear the old songs, including Patsy Cline's "Life's Railway to Heaven." I am wearing a house dress and enjoying straightening chairs, sweeping floors and polishing counters.

While I work, I think of my parents and I think about my grandparents. I think about our history and our way of life. I think about the example of hard work, throughout the generations, as a shining example of old fashioned families.

There is so much history in homemaking. As we go through each day, ironing, folding laundry, baking, washing windows and sweeping floors, we become a **living museum** of the old days - the days when *home was everything*. May we continue to be a witness, of a precious era, to a dying world.

Kitchen Sermons

The past few days, I have been listening to sermons while working in the kitchen. I love taking my time, polishing the counters and washing dishes and listening to an inspiring sermon.

Each day I have chosen one sermon to enjoy. I have heard Dr. John MacArthur talk about the economy; Dr. Harold Sightler describe the blessings of all the food fed to thousands just from one small lunch, in "*What Are They Among So Many?*" I had tears in my eyes as Dr. Clyde Box preached on "*A Faithful Man, Who can Find?*" A few of these ministers are southern, and will *shout* at times. It certainly startles me out of a spiritual sloth!

Sometimes the children will walk into the room while I am working. They want to talk, so I pause the sermon. I listen to the children and then turn the CD back on. The preaching echoes throughout the house. It is like propaganda in the home - **good propaganda** that nourishes the soul.

The endless daily chores in the kitchen are ideal times for listening to sermons. Knowing there is something special to listen to while I work makes me eager to do my duties.

Mother's Labors

I was thinking about the old days, when Mothers were always at home. Every mother in the neighborhood would be doing laundry, harvesting the garden or tending to babies. Children ran and played while the mothers looked on.

There were even older mothers who had grown children, but still remained at home. These mothers still had porches to sweep, laundry to do, and dishes to wash. These mothers still had homes they were responsible for.

All the mothers had to shop in the market to stock their kitchens. These mothers used family recipes, passed down through the generations, to cook for their families. They also used a trusted Betty Crocker cookbook.

These women were **diligent** and **dependable**.

Any time a neighbor was in need, a mother was always home to help - A Mother who knew pain and struggle and sacrifice, because she lived in the trenches of home-life.

Sadly, somewhere along the line, mother's labors were diminished in the eyes of society. Mother was replaced by fast food restaurants and processed foods. Any child with a microwave could prepare his own lunch. Any husband could go to the drive through and order his dinner. There was no more comfort food. There was no more sacrifice and love in the presentation of mealtimes. The *thanks* and the *memories* went to take-out places and companies who produced canned goods.

Society started to think that sloth was "in," and cleanliness was unnecessary. Wrinkled clothes were part of a new era of being casual. The irons sat *un-used* on closet shelves.

Walking into an *empty* home. . . one that lacked a Mother cooking in the kitchen at supper time . . . was a normal sight. Nobody was home to greet the family.

Many mothers headed off into the land of rush, rush, rush, and hurry, hurry, hurry. The neighborhoods became empty. Somehow, *someway*, society forgot that creating a godly home required the steady efforts of Mother's old fashioned labor.

Is Mother at Home?

It takes a lot of effort to make a happy home. We mothers deal with trials and moods within our families. We have lots of housework, planning and errands to attend to. We also must keep our spiritual lives in order.

Spiritual duties of Bible reading, prayer, listening to hymns (or singing them) and spiritual songs are what help to nourish our souls. These are required on a **daily basis** to help keep the toxic world around us from causing us harm.

I read this beautiful analogy from the 1800's book, *"Aunt Jane's Hero."* She described a yearning for Heaven, that had to do with wanting to be with Jesus. It wasn't about the siblings, babies or loved ones that went on before us. While being with those precious people again is our goal, we are seeking the eternal presence of Jesus because He is the foundation of it all; and the sweetness that we crave. The author of *"Aunt Jane's Hero,"* compared this with a child who comes home. He walks in the door and calls out, **"Is Mother at Home?"** If he finds that mother is there, he is content and secure and happy. It doesn't matter if Daddy is there or if siblings are there, for they may come home soon. But the center of the home - Mother - the shining light of it all, is what brings the sweet, relieved smile. *This is the presence we yearn to go home to.*

I want to be just like that Mother. But I fail miserably. I want everyone to come home and say, "Is Mother here?" And I want them to smile and seek me out. I want to provide them with selfless love and servant-hood to bring them great joy in our humble home.

The Kitchen Martyr

I was just scrubbing my dimly-lit kitchen tonight. It was so pleasant in there. Yet I am tired and worn out from a long day. As I cleaned, a calmness came over me. I was listening to *Clair De Lune* on CD. It made me think of being a Kitchen Martyr. (gentle smiles) I worked and slaved in the kitchen, but enjoyed it tremendously because the music comforted and soothed me. When I was finished, I looked around at the pleasant rooms - my kitchen and my parlour. Everything was put back "to rights," and looked lovely. All the work was worth it.

I read somewhere that housewives in the 1960's spent an average of 4 hours a day cleaning their homes, compared to 2 hours a day for modern housewives. I was amazed. I realize that mothers are often ill, or they are very busy, but if we could fit in more housework in our days, we would really enjoy the effort and the result.

I will leave you with this thought from Mathew Henry - *"It is the duty of those who have the charge of families to look well to the ways of their household. The affectation of state and the love of ease make many families neglected."* **The love of ease**, is something I am constantly fighting against!

Preparations for Homekeeping

In the early morning hours, I sit in a dim room thinking about the day. I often read, sip on tea or listen to some quiet music. It is a lovely time to prepare for my homekeeping work.

I have so much to worry and fret about, but I won't indulge in such emotions. I refuse to give up or give-in to trouble.

I will bake some bread to go with tonight's supper.

I will do laundry, sweep, scrub, and clean the kitchen throughout the day.

I will bake apple cinnamon muffins for the children's snack.

I will listen to a sermon by Charles Stanley about Motherhood.

And then, whenever I can spare a few moments, I will sit in a dimly lit room and think pleasant thoughts about good literature, sermons, classical music, tea time and other inspiring ideas. This will prepare me for the evening duties.

Refusing to worry about the myriad trials I have each day, will help keep things running smoothly for everyone around me. . . *And if I get a little sad, I will read some comic books.*

If Home was a Happy Place

Many suffer every day because of sorrow, depression and trials. They have trouble coping. This happens to teens, mothers, fathers and young adults. It seems that *small children* are more carefree, and innocent of the dark- clouds in life.

Homes are very precious when they are full of young children to brighten everyone's mood!

We Mothers have the weight of the world on our shoulders when we try to create joy and happiness at home without our spiritual strength. If we can "seek ye first the kingdom of God and his righteousness" the Lord will help us. It will seem almost **effortless** as His light shines through us.

When you are having a rough time at home, perhaps your teens are angry and moody? Or perhaps your husband is on edge and stressed? Just remember this - instead of thinking about how to solve the problems, or trying out different ideas to make things better - simply spend more time in private prayer, bible reading and letting God worry about it all.

Because if our homes are going to be happy places, in this ungodly world, we need the constant source of light coming through our souls. No human effort will make it work. *We need The Lord.*

Mother, have you hugged your Bible today?

What Time Does Your Shift Start?

If homekeeping is an occupation, do we have a time of day when we start work? Do we get ready and dressed in a specific uniform or professional outfit, like a dress and apron? Do we look pretty for our job? Pretty and Presentable?

I was reading a "*Good Old Days*" book, set during the great depression. GIs were coming home from the war and heading to college. Many of them were married and needed housing for their small families. One man found an old house near a school. He rented a room from the owner. He described the house as run down and dirty. The Landlady had been a wealthy woman, but all her servants had left to find work elsewhere. This woman told her tenants that she had never done menial labor in her life, and wasn't about to start now! (smiles)

Is housework menial labor? Or is it honest work?

I recently watched a movie where there was a wealthy family. They had a full-time maid. Well, the maid came into some money. She was encouraged to quit her job. The maid wondered *why*? She loved what she did and was proud of her work. She was skilled and did an excellent job. Why would she quit? I was so inspired by her attitude!

Homemakers should be proud of their work too. Not only are we cleaning and cooking, but we are caring for our own possessions - our homes! This should help us to get into a good daily routine. We should take our jobs seriously and do our very best.

If you started work at 8 a.m., would you be dressed and ready? I know we homemakers are available to work 24 hours a day - just like many doctors, right? But if we took pride in our work and made that extra effort to show up for our shift on time, and prepared, things would run more smoothly and pleasant.

When Mr. White and I owned a country store, I would get up every morning before 5 a.m. I had to be ready all day long, until around 11 p.m - just in case I was needed. So I would be nicely dressed and on-call. Sometimes I would have to head across the street to the store, with the children, to help him for a little while. So I had to be ready. In my mind, my shift started at 6 a.m. and ended at 11 p.m. During those hours, I was ready and presentable.

Being a homemaker can have starting shifts. We can also joke about it with our children. After bedtime hours, a teenager might ask a question or want to have a late night snack. We mothers could look at our watches (or pretend we have a watch on) and say, "*Well, my shift ends in 30 minutes, so I have a little time to help you with that.*" When I say this to my older children, they are amused! But the truth is, we need breaks and we need a stopping point. Perhaps that is 8 p.m. or maybe it is 11 p.m. It depends on your family situation. But certainly set in your mind a starting shift and a time when you are finished.

Maybe all the regular work will be done, or almost done by the end of the shift, and Mom can rest!

What Kind of Queen are You?

I've heard the saying about "*Mother*" being "Queen of Her Home." This sets in my mind an image of pampered luxury. I imagine her reverenced by all. I see her as being famous and much admired. I see her as living a life of ease.

I think there is a serious danger in this mind-set. Because it can make us feel spoiled and ill-prepared for the reality of our work.

This is what it is like for Mothers:

1. Lack of sleep.

2. Cleaning up spills and carelessly-left messes.

3. Going without / always sacrificing.

4. Constantly fighting our own self-will so we properly care for our children (rather than always thinking about "me").

5. Forgiving every little slight and flaw to keep peace in the home.

6. Working despite pain. Working despite trials. Working despite danger.

When I think of a Queen, I imagine Queen Elizabeth of England. She has tremendous concern for Britain. She is dignified, private, the essence of poise and manners, and unflinchingly dedicated to her role and duties.

I also think of Queen Esther in Scripture. She thought of her people. She did her job without asking for perks, pampering or luxury.

Personally, I cannot bear the thought of thinking of myself as "Queen" of my home, because I already have a tendency to be spoiled, seeking ease, and wanting to be waited on. I am nothing like Queen Elizabeth or Queen Esther, though I dearly wish I had an ounce of their characters. Instead, I have to think of myself as lowly, humble and "not much." Because truly, if I am not "The Servant" of this house, if I am not the lowly housewife who has to do common labor, how will I ever learn to be "the least among them."

Creating a Pleasant Atmosphere at Home

In the early afternoon, I start making preparations for the comfort of my husband and teenagers. I lay out refreshments on the kitchen counter. These are neatly arranged treats and vary by - day, depending on whether or not I baked, or found a sale at the market. Often, there will be a bakery coffee cake, some cookies, fresh bread and fruit. There may even be some cake or brownies. I usually have 2 or 3 different choices waiting for my hungry family to enjoy.

Next, I tidy up the parlour table. This is just our dining room table, since we don't have an eat-in kitchen. On this table, I lay out a box of Checkers, and a pack of playing cards. At any time, my teenagers can walk by and say, "*Hey, who wants to play a game?*" Some days, I put out Yahtzee or Boggle. I need to get a new game of Scrabble. That would provide a nice variety.

These mere acts of housekeeping are often what people only do when they are expecting guests to visit. However, it is something we can do for our families on a daily basis.

Once I set up the games and the refreshments, I will put on some classical music while I do some cleaning. Then I head off to read before it is time to start making dinner.

How a Housewife Passes the Time

We've all read scores of stories about homemakers who had "work baskets." These contained knitting and mending projects, or some kind of embroidery. Women would carry these with them when visiting friends. They would also keep them in the parlour for when they had a break from housekeeping. They would work with their hands to be productive while they passed the time.

One of my favorite things to do is read. I have scholarly books, fun books, and instructive books. I also have some Charlie Brown Comics, which make me smile. One in particular, *"PEANUTS TREASURY,"* was published in 1968, and contains comics from the 50's and 60's. There are two charming comics in there that are adorable, because they provide for us a glimpse to the past. Young Sally (Charlie's sister) is worried about going to school for the first time. She bolts up in bed and says something like, *"When I grow up, I want to be a housewife . . . Why should I have to go to Kindergarten?"* In another comic, she talks about how she has no interest in learning new math, because she has no need for that as a future housewife. While a future housewife should certainly go to school and learn math and other skills, I loved how innocent Sally was about it all. I also love the way girls were encouraged, at that time, to aspire to be housewives.

I have to find another good book to enjoy today. I will place it on the little table beside my chair in the parlour. I usually sit over there, near the window, and drink my tea. I will read when I finish my kitchen duties. The house is generally quiet at this time of day. Reading makes for a pleasant way to start the day.

Later, as it gets colder here in Vermont, I will find a hand-sewing project to work on while I sit by the fire. I have no idea what I will make. It will probably be a small quilt. It doesn't really matter. The fun is in the sewing and being available to talk and laugh with the family while I work. It is a restful, peaceful routine for the winter.

Domestic Incentives

We all have our off-days when we don't want to do anything. Why is it that we need motivation to do our housework? I remember telling myself, one early morning when I didn't want to get out of bed, "If Mr. White gave you $500 and said, *'go shopping today and buy anything you want.'*" I would **promptly** get up, with lots of energy. So it has to be a "mood" when we don't feel like being productive at home.

I remember reading one of Erma Bombeck's books and she was talking about this (in the 1960's). She said one housewife treated herself to a cocktail at 9 in the morning just for making the coffee.

Why do we need incentives? Perhaps because we are surrounded by a culture where few seem to care about homemaking. It is something we have to fight against each day. So if you need to have a cookie as a reward for doing the laundry - go right ahead!

The Vision of Home

Temptations, Invitations and Urgings keep trying to call me away from home. They keep trying to get mother away from keeping the home.

There is so much tranquility here. It is a slow - paced kind of life, when Mother is always at home. She is able to cook and bake and clean. She is able to pray and spend time with her family.

The other day, I was working in the kitchen and getting so much accomplished. I made several batches of suppers for the freezer. This was for those rough days when I needed to rest, or focus on other things. But I needed to stay home and have the strength to finish my work.

I remember someone mentioning Nehemiah in the Bible and how he could not come down from the wall, because he was doing God's work. Was something trying to call him away?

I don't want my home to fall in ruins because I did not have a heart for it. I have a calling to be **here**. *Please, don't tempt me, or distract me away from my work.*

What a great blessing it is to have a vision of home. It is not only a vision but a dedicated heart. It is a form of heaven on earth - an artistic endeavor in hospitality, and of creating the beauty of a traditional family.

Classy Homemaking

Whenever my Mother had to go out, she would put on a little lipstick. Then she would go to her bureau and dab a little perfume on her neck and wrists. This was a way to be refreshed and prepare to be sociable outside the home, on her errands, or for appointments.

Mother always looked nice, though, even at home. Her hair was always done. Her clothes were pretty and neat. She enjoyed her daily tasks and always made good food for us to enjoy.

Lately, I have been a little out of sorts. Early in the morning, I put on my apron, fix my hair and . . . then I remember that my pearl necklace is missing. I always love to put that on when I am cleaning the house. It is like getting dressed up to do my work. The necklace is just a $20 piece of jewelry but it makes me happy. Still, it almost feels like I am missing something. I am without that little piece of *class* that helps me take pride in my work at home.

Nevertheless, there are plenty of ways we can add a little style to our homemaking. How about getting a fresh flower from the garden and putting that in your hair? Join that with a little happy step and soon, cleaning the house will be a way to keep you cheerful! I mean, what fun is it to put on some old sloppy clothes and drudge through our home duties? We can make a little extra effort, with lipstick, pearls, fixing our hair and even flowers - to help us with our work. Imagine how our family would feel seeing us look classy while we kept house? That would inspire them and make them appreciate home even more.

The Old Sunday Dinner

In the Old Days, American Families would gather round the table after Church for a big Sunday dinner. Often relatives would come by - like a brother, aunt or cousins. There would be laughter and happiness and a joyous day of rest from labor. There were Blue laws * so the stores were all closed. It was like the country encouraged everyone to stay home and have family time. This was still going on in the 1960's.

Mother went out of her way to plan and prepare a hearty meal. She would get the children to help her set the table and then send them off so they would not be "under foot." Mother made a big pitcher of lemonade or iced tea. She also had plenty of freshly brewed coffee. There was often fresh baked bread, or biscuits, that she had prepared the day before. This big meal was a way to nourish the family with *comfort* and *love*.

After dinner, the women visited and cleaned up. Sometimes they talked about the state of the culture or comforted each other over some trial. This helped make getting through the week much better, knowing they would get together each Sunday after Church.

The men would head outdoors or in the living room and talk and visit, while the children raced out to the porch, or the back field, to enjoy each other's company.

For The Love of Christian Homemaking

This was a precious time of remembering the morning sermon, refreshing the soul with good fellowship and enjoying a rest from worldly cares.

I think we lost a little something when the blue laws were mostly repealed.

The Blue Laws were In Effect in Massachusetts, where I grew up, and where my Mother grew up. Other states had similar laws.

A Break That is Deserved

There have been times I wanted to rest all day and do *nothing*. Those days leave me feeling guilty, bored and ill. There is a reason we need to work. We need to *deserve* our rest. We need to earn it.

Imagine treating homemaking as a beautiful art project. We are busy for most of the day, creating a delightful, inviting home. Perhaps we are outdoors hanging clothes on the line and then we work in the garden. We may gather fresh fruit and freshly cut flowers and bring these into the home to brighten and cheer our families.

Perhaps we are busy repainting an old chair on the front porch. Maybe we sweep and dust and polish the bedrooms. Next, we may open windows to let in all the fresh air. And maybe this was all done just after sun-up!

Now we have an entire day to enjoy! We deserve a break! It is time to sit in the parlour and sip on lemonade. It is time to enjoy a book or a little hand embroidery while visiting with family and guests.

After this time of refreshment, we are back to our project - *the making and keeping of home*. We are content and happy with our work. We begin preparing a special lunch. Our mood is calm. We are not in a state of hurry or stress. We have paced ourselves and accomplished lovely things. But we also indulged in a peaceful time of rest!

Next, the family gathers at home with all their news and excitement of the day. We have a wonderful supper ready. We have spent time reading the Bible and listening to gospel music while we worked. We are ready for the *night hour*. This is a peaceful time. We tidy the kitchen by candlelight and listen to soothing classical music. We are dressed in our finest apron and present ourselves as a vision of meekness and beauty.

The Home is clean. The family is rested. It is time to for family prayers and thanksgiving. It is time to shut off the lights, close the curtains and enjoy the coziness of a happy home.

Homemaking Survival

There are certain things we have to do each day, no matter how we feel about it. We have to cook and clean and make sure there is food in the pantry. Sometimes we are so exhausted that we complain or even indulge in crying. This is not the way the old-time homemakers lived.

Many Immigrant mothers came to America with strong backbones. They were used to hard work and ran their homes with dignity and courage. They were not fazed by trials. They knew to pray to God for help, and then got right to work. These homemakers did not give in to their emotions like many of us do today. (I only *wish* I were as strong as they were!)

My grandmother was in a wheelchair for most of her adult life, but she ran her home with great strength of character and an unbending value system. Her morals were strong and she passed those on to her children.

If the task of homemaking is going to survive, we need hard working mothers who do their job each day despite the trouble and trials that constantly attack us.

Sometimes, the trials are from our own children. Often teenagers and young adults don't want to walk the old paths. This can make us almost want to give up and die...... But we must keep going. We must smile as often as we can and live the godly life and find our joy and strength from the Lord. No matter what anyone around us is doing, we must continue with our work.

For the past couple of days, I have been in a lot of pain and unable to do much. This morning, I am much better and ready to face the family and my chores with new zeal. Today, I will work for a couple of hours and I will plan nice meals. Then I will read my Bible and rest.

Making the Morning Pleasant for the Family

The sun is just now rising. The house is warm and cozy. The family is still sleeping. This is the quiet time of the morning kitchen. This is the time to start the coffee, or make the tea, and begin the housework. Pull out your best china cup and have your favorite hot drink while you work!

I will be making chocolate chip muffins today. I will get right to work in just a little while. The aroma of freshly baked muffins and coffee in the morning will help cheer up the family.

I have some errands to do and other adventures to accomplish. This is my *to-do* list. Instead of writing what I have to do, at the top of the page, I write "Today's Adventures!" and then write my list. It is all in the attitude! Our morning will go smoothly despite any grumpy- morning- people, if I am cheerful and prepared for a happy morning.

There are other ways to brighten the day for the family. Last month, Mr. White bought a cute little stuffed elephant. He set it on the kitchen table in Amy's (16) spot. When she woke up, she walked into the room, spotted the elephant and her eyes widened. She smiled and said, "*Is this for me?*" She was so happy. It really helped make her day pleasant.

Amy told me later that she thinks everyone's day should start with a *little elephant*.

Cooking While Holding a Bible

There is plenty of work to do in this house. All day long I cooked. . . and cleaned. . . and cared for the children. All day long I took care of everyone else and struggled with my lack of benevolence. *"I can only do so much!"* - I constantly prayed to the Lord. . . And yes, I fell asleep for 20 minutes in the afternoon and had trouble snapping out of it when I was needed again. But I kept going. . .

I kept working on making a home and feeding the family. I had my hair up and looked as nice as I could through it all. Does *haggard beauty* count for something?

Evening came. I did dishes and then started supper. But it was getting late. I did not want to miss our Bible time. So John (13) and I pulled out the Bibles. . . and hymn books . . . and my record book*. We said the prayers. I got up to stir the hamburger. We sang *Rock of Ages*, from memory, while I worked. Then I sat back down to take turns reading the Bible.

Supper needed to be cooked. Yet, I would not neglect our worship time. So I grabbed my Bible and held it in one hand, while I stirred the supper. . . I took my turn reading, and following along with John.

The light of the stove was dim in our old kitchen. The steam of the food was warm. The work was hard. But I held that Bible and continued to cook. No one was there to see our faithfulness. But God saw. And it was precious.

The record book is where I keep track of our bible times.

For The Love of Christian Homemaking

An Elegant Home Despite Poverty

Sometimes, my house seems beat-up and old. Well, it is old! It was built in 1850 for a lawyer who had a wife and 10 children. When we first bought this house, I went to the memorial museum of our small town and searched the history. I also bought some old books which were written by residents many years ago. I saw old pictures and enjoyed reading their history.

All around me I see wealth and beauty in classy, new homes. I see elegance and distinction. Then I look at my own estate and see the house needs a paint job and the porch steps are falling apart. I am reminded of my life as the old country wife who lives in poverty - like in the movie "*The Dollmaker,* "starring Jane Fonda. Didn't that one just make you cry? Or what about the mother of Loretta Lynn in "*Coal Miner's Daughter?* " Those are the women I relate to - The hardworking mothers of humble means.

I was just looking at some photographs of my house. I see holes in my kitchen linoleum. But the floors are shiny and clean in the sunlight. I see an old country kitchen, but it is pretty and tidy. I see walls in desperate need of a paint job - but there are children smiling and happy, playing cards or laughing, in the photographs.

I go about my day in an apron and dress. I clean and tidy and make this place a home. To me, it is a home of elegance. It is a precious place I love, and take pride in. Even though my furniture is old and second-hand, it clearly speaks of an old fashioned, creative homemaker.

The Evening Hour at Home

The house is dim and quiet. I am doing some dishes and getting things tidied up for a peaceful night. I am listening to gospel music and enjoying my housework. The stove is roaring and cozy in the living room. I will sit in a comfortable chair and rest for a bit. Then I will finish some laundry and cleaning projects.

I would like to bake a special treat for the family to enjoy. It will either be a cake or some cookies. I think a cake will be easier. I have a vanilla cake mix and some vanilla frosting for a nice change of pace. This is a favorite flavor for some of the men in the family.

Our kitchen is very dim. Our overhead light is blown out. We will not bother to replace it any time soon. I am using a small light above my stove for now. The fun part is getting all my heavy cleaning and cooking finished before the sun sets. Otherwise it is too dark in there to accomplish much. My dimly lit kitchen reminds me of the old days. People would work from sun-up to sun-down. Then they would rest and read by lamp-light. It was quieter in those day. When lights are bright, it makes home a little too "noisy" for me. I like the soft, gentle light on a cold winter night.

As soon as I finish my work, I will rest content, knowing my labors of the day were well done.

Going to Meeting

The capable housewives from the 1930's and 1940's would have all their housework and baking finished and they would go to "meeting." These dear ladies went to the old revival meetings at church. They went to the church picnics and church services.

These ladies would not even consider staying home with an excuse like, *"I don't feel good,"* or *"I won't have time to make supper."* I am inspired by their legacy as I am getting ready to go to a church event tonight despite feeling tired and weary. At this moment, is my house clean enough? Is the supper made? Have I done the laundry? Well, since I have been ill since yesterday afternoon, I haven't done much more than direct the children to do the basic necessities. I am trying not to give in to the urge of crying since I cannot overexert myself with my regular chores. But will I give up and stay home tonight, or will I go to meeting? Clearly, I will hold my head up and attend church tonight with my family. I will pray for strength and I will try to get a little bit of work done before I leave. I will not be a slacker housewife! I will not complain and wish my children did more or that I had a maid.

I remember my southern Aunt. She was the wife of a preacher. My Uncle had a wonderful church in rural Alabama. I remember staying at their house and seeing how much work she did at home. She baked food from scratch, gardened, cleaned her house, entertained us with her her charming southern conversations and went to all the church meetings with us. She would wear regular clothes at home, then get all dressed up for church . . . Just like the wives and mothers from the 1930's and 1940's! She was a real-life example to me.

The Neglected Parlour

Our cozy parlour is cold and dreary today. We are conserving the last of our wood pellets until Friday when Mr. White will buy a ton for the month. Little wonder the room has been neglected. I dearly miss sitting in my favorite chair reading "*Dombey and Son*" by Charles Dickens. The book is almost 1,000 pages long and I am halfway through. It is such a treasure!

I have spent much of the day resting and trying to recover from ongoing illnesses. I keep taking "cleaning" breaks. In other words. I take a break from resting so I can clean for a few minutes at a time. (smiles).

In just a few days our little room will be warm again and I will be back in my chair and enjoying my book. So for now, the dream of reading and resting near the fire will have to be good enough.

Delicate Beauty of Homemaking

I have been watching old episodes of *Little House on the Prairie* today and thinking about a quiet life at home. Ma Ingalls would sit by the fire at night, in her rocking chair, and do the mending. She would look up and smile at her family as they talked or played nearby. During the day, she was busy baking bread, cleaning or tending to her flowers, or garden, around the front property.

Home was quiet. It was a pleasant place to be. We need more Ma Ingalls who are sweet and meek and gentle but who will work hard at home. I know we mothers get very tired at times, but we must do our home duties. We need to work hard to make home a precious place. We need to find pretty things and create and decorate.

Regardless of the trials and tribulations we endure, we can make the meals; We can cook and bake and clean and present security in our routines. Trials and sorrows will pass, but Mother's cheerful labors will inspire us all. Homemakers are the light of the home. They are the creators of delicate culture. Their gentle, loving influence reaches far and wide.

A Jane Austen Day

[When Mother is Worn Out]

I have been struggling to keep up with the errands and daily life. Last night, I didn't think I could continue. I needed to just lay down and have the day over. But I prayed and washed the dishes and then laid down for an hour. I prayed for strength. We had a Church meeting I did not want to miss. It is funny how whenever I get involved in such an amazing ministry program that something tries to get in the way of my involvement. After a couple of hours, I was refreshed and energized and we went to the meeting. It was such a blessing! The children and I came back with renewed zeal and plenty of ministry ideas.

This morning, I woke up and did my exercises, but something happened. My weariness came back. I decided that I need a break. I will not give in to this and be sad or miserable. I will make this rest fun. I will liven up my spirit with a pleasant idea. I will have a Jane Austen Day! What does that mean?

I will dress in a delicate outfit - a pretty long dress. I will fix my hair and settle myself near the hearth all day long and read "*Emma.*" I will relax and think of my home as a "cottage," and enjoy a life of delicate leisure at home while I recover, listening to gentle classical music.

Suppertime in a Rural Home

It is getting dark. The day is almost over. Mama is wearing her apron and cooking in the kitchen. She's smiling and happy and humming a tune, while she leans over the stove.

The children come in from their play. They are cold and excited and talking about all the snowmen they created. Such sweet smiles on their faces! Their eyes light up when they enter the warm house. They put away their coats and settle down to wait for supper.

Daddy walks in after a hard day at work. He is tired. But all his troubles seem to melt away when he enters the inviting rural home.

Some of the children help Mama set the table. They lay out plates and silverware, cups and napkins. Another child comes over to pour drinks. The table looks inviting.

Mama brings out platters of food. She serves fresh warm bread, butter, stew and salad. The children are hungry and excited to enjoy a nice meal with the family.

They sit around the table. Dad says the prayer. Everyone is thankful and smiling. If you are walking by, on that cold winter night, and you happen to see them through the window, you will see laughter and smiles. You will see a happy family eating their supper and full of love and gratefulness.

Mama cleans up while the children run off to play. They are getting their baths and will soon hear a bedtime story. Mama is humming while she washes dishes and polishes the table. Life inside that home is peaceful and joyous. The outside cares and troubles fade away, when it's suppertime in the old rural house.

Early Morning Dew

I just hung the clothes on the line. The world is just waking up and the air is cool and crisp. The grass is covered with the early morning dew.

It is quiet here. There is a stillness during this time of day. I do a little housework and take the time to walk out on the porch to look at the landscape. Then I get my tea and sit with a good book until the family begins to stir.

I am in a serene mood. But I know it won't last. The household will get loud, there will be more chores than I can manage and the world will awaken.

But I can have this quiet time again tomorrow. Each morning I strive to wake up earlier and earlier so it will last longer.

A Place They Want to Come Home To

The kitchen is the center of the home. When guests come by, a Homemaker always offers a refreshment - food or drink. Sometimes a guest will decline. This is when the Homemaker begins to *coax*:

"I just baked an apple pie and we have vanilla ice cream to go with it. Wouldn't you like some?

There is a sparkle in the eyes of the guest. They enjoy the delightful treat and have a pleasant visit.

This is the same with our husband and children. They love to hear Mother say, *"Can I make you something special to eat?"*

This is what I was thinking about last night. It was 4:30 in the afternoon and I didn't know what I was going to make for supper. I wanted everyone to have a lovely evening. I wanted supper to be a family event. I wanted to make sure they always wanted to come home.

So I began working on the environment. I put on my apron and turned on soothing Classical music to inspire me. Here is what I did:

1. I cleared off and washed the kitchen table. (The children had been playing cards earlier.)

2. I placed a vanilla scented candle in the center and then lit it.

I still didn't know what was for supper.

3. I pulled some burger out of the freezer to begin to defrost.

4. I set the table. I used Styrofoam (paper) plates. I put out napkins and forks. I put a glass at every plate.

5. I went in the kitchen and prepared carrot sticks. Then I sliced up some Cracker Barrel Cheddar Cheese and placed these on a small serving plate. Both items were carefully and artfully placed on the table.

6. I found the salt and pepper shakers and put them on the table.

I still didn't know what was for supper.

7. I made a large batch of iced tea and put this in the fridge to chill.

8. I saw one of the children walk through, take some cheese, smile, and then run off.

9. I started to fry up the burger. I added a bit of water to the pan to slow down the cooking, giving it more time to defrost and to prevent burning.

I knew what was for supper.

10. I started to boil water to make egg noodles.

11. I pulled out bread crumbs, garlic powder, vegetable oil, cheddar and mozzarella cheese. Everything would be mixed up together to make a sort of homemade hamburger helper.

12. I warmed English muffins in the toaster oven and then buttered and sliced them in half. These were laid out artfully on a serving plate.

When the food was all finished, I placed it on the table with serving spoons. I called the children for supper. As they sat down, I said:

"Use your best table manners."

I listened as the children talked and laughed while helping themselves to food. When someone began to talk about something I didn't like, I would say, *"Not of general interest!"* (This lovely phrase is from the 1940's book, *"Cheaper by the Dozen"* by the Gilbreth family.) This helps keep the conversation appropriate and interesting for everyone.

After Amy (15) finished eating, she lingered at the table. She was smiling and enjoying our company. She did not run off. I was delighted and I *noticed*. It was a pleasant meal.

This is the kind of place they will want to come home to. It takes effort to create a pleasant environment for the family. But in the process, I am rewarded beyond measure.

The Old Time Mothers

When I was a young girl, I remember dreaming about having an old house. I imagined a large front porch, peeling paint, and a simple home. This was the reality for the Old Time Mothers. They lived in cabins on the Prairie, or small homes on farms.

Their houses were clean and these mothers worked hard preparing meals to feed their families. There was no television, no computer, no phone, and no malls. Life centered around the family, hard work, and godliness.

These mothers did not complain. They were too busy to worry about 'self-help,' or what they were 'missing out on.' These saints of old depended on God and prayed often. They had great faith for all their needs. They were blessed beyond measure.

I cannot imagine seeing a dusty Bible in a home like that.

Holiness from the Garage

I love walking into an old-time church. The congregation is often a humble, kind group who are there to join together in prayer and worship. These kinds of churches are hard to find, but they are such a blessing!

I think about these churches when my Father (Grandpa) is out working on the property. He is in his 70's and keeps busy maintaining the grounds and doing repair projects. He has full possession of our two-car garage. He uses it as a workshop. There is a wood stove in there, counters, and tools. He also has a cassette player and 8 track player. (*He, along with Nana, live in their own section of our large old house.*)

Throughout the day, I can hear the *sounds of holiness coming from the garage.* Grandpa plays old gospel music or old sermons of his brother preaching. It gives me a warm feeling of comfort. *I am safe here* because of Grandpa. I go about my housekeeping with the windows open, and I can hear the precious sounds of worship and spiritual nourishment. It awakens me to live a holy life. It protects me from worldly distractions. It is a testimony that says, *Grandpa is here.*

In my section of the house, I am often listening to sermons or old gospel music. I read my Bible and pray and delight in spiritual duties. I am continuing Grandpa's tradition and passing it on to the next generation. As my children age and mature, they will be drawn to this kind of life. They will be drawn to the peace and joy which comes from religious duties. It is the legacy of holiness.

Sweet Hours at Home

Evening at home is a lovely time, even in the most humble home. The housewife might be mending by the fire, smiling at the children while they play. Father is reading the paper, and sharing a bit of news that may interest his little brood.

The family has had their supper, and finished their nightly chores. They enjoy some time in the warm room, forgetting the day's troubles.

The world is shut out. The day is done. These are sweet hours on the home front.

Soon it is time for family prayers. . . The Bible is read. Prayers are said. Then each one is tucked into a warm bed.

Another precious day has become a beautiful memory.

Early Winter Morning

In the early dawn of a winter morning, mothers would start a fire in the wood stove. This helped warm the house and prepared the stove for cooking the family breakfast.

Mother might walk outdoors in the snow to gather wood from the wood box. This was a peaceful time of day, when the sun was just rising and the air was calm and quiet. She might look around at the beauty of the landscape.

Then she would come indoors and prepare the coffee and tea. She would bake the biscuits and fry up the meat, or stir up some oatmeal. The scent from the kitchen and the crackling of the fire helped to slowly awaken the family.

Each would wash up and do their chores and then sit down together for the morning meal. They had their prayer and time of devotion and then each would attend to their tasks.

This quiet, pleasant, winter morning is something many of us *crave*. Yet, we are bombarded by the distractions of noise and technology.

Perhaps if we found a way to enjoy the *silence* of a winter morning, and did old fashioned preparations for the day, we would find some peace and courage to manage in this stressful world.

"Dear Kitchen"

Late yesterday afternoon (after a prolonged illness) I walked into my messy kitchen with a look of joy on my face. I was so happy to be up and moving around again. I said, out loud, (**to my kitchen**), "*Did you miss me?*"

I had the most lovely time washing dishes, cleaning the counter and sweeping the floor. I did a little polishing but then got tired. I slowly tidied up the parlour, looked around at the rooms and sighed with relief and contentment.

I was delighted to have been able to clean again.

"My Home Library"

After I am dead, my children will search through the hundreds of books in my home library. Then they will find all the empty wrappers of m and m candy that I have used as bookmarks.

Nana in Alabama

My Father's mother lived in rural Alabama. We called her "Nana in Alabama" because we lived with our Mother's mother, who was our resident Nana (in Massachusetts). I loved them both dearly.

Nana in the old south was a legend in my eyes. She was the sweetest, gentlest lady in the world. We visited her once a year for a few weeks at a time. I heard all kinds of stories about her. She was married to revival preacher (LD Murphy) and had seven children. Only two lived to be adults - my father, and his brother, my Uncle Bobby who was a precious preacher. His sermons tore me up and made me weep every time.

Nana had a lot of trials in her life. A lot of heartbreak. Her Mother died when she was a young teenager. She dropped out of school and took care of her older brothers and father. She kept house for them. When her father died shortly thereafter, she married my Grandpa. He was an incredible man. He was dedicated to the Lord and to his family. They struggled financially but were always taken care of. When their youngest son (my father) was 16 years old, Grandpa (his dad) died. That boy was so heartbroken. So devastated.... he went on to support and take care of his mother. He worked and provided for her while she kept house, working hard at home.

Nana had a special hymn that she loved to sing. It was called "Farther Along." It talked about being Tempted and Tried, and how we'll understand it all by and by. And we are to "cheer up our brother" and "live in the sunshine."

When I was a young teenager, my father taught me that song. I had never heard it anywhere, except by his singing it to me. I learned all the words and have sung it myself all these years. I always think of her and her struggles in life and her amazing faith in the Lord. And I cry...........

Making the Most of Home

Did you ever see that movie, *"The Dollmaker,"* starring Jane Fonda? It is the saddest, sweetest, most educational movie I have ever seen. It encourages you to be extremely thrifty, and a hardworking, loving Mother. I will never forget seeing Jane's character moving into an apartment that she didn't want to be in. Her husband made a decision she hated, but she left her little rented house in the country and moved into this little place. The very first thing she did was get on her knees and scrub the floors. She was going to make the best of things.

There are all kinds of homes - apartments, condos, mobile homes, and houses. Some are old and worn out. Some are generally dirtier and in need of repairs, while others are clean, and new. Whether we live in a state of almost poverty or with wealth, we have to make the most of what we have.

Through our attitude and plenty of hard work, we can make our homes look clean and pleasant. Add to that a loving, tender smile to brighten the hearts of our family and guests, and home will be a sweet and precious place.

Pretty Things to Cheer Me Up

Today has been one of those days. It is chilly and raining and *depressing*. . . No matter what I did, nothing could make me smile. I even tried resting, eating cookies, praying and washing dishes (smiles). But none of that helped. I finally realized I need some pretty things around me to cheer me up. I need to help create a better mood. No one else can do that for me.

So in just a little while, I will put on my burgundy, ruffled apron - the elegant one. And I will put on some *Mozart*. I will light a candle and do a little tidying in my kitchen. I like to *clean a house* that is **already** clean - because it is far more pleasant to tidy things and polish things, than to have to work on a horrid mess.

I will clean as I go. And I will start an elegant supper. I will be happy and smile and be cheerful, while I sip on tea. *It will be a lovely night.*

Daydreaming about Housekeeping

There are times when we will just sit and plan all the things we need to do in a day. We might make long lists of chores, and baking projects. We might even get some of those things accomplished.

But have you ever *daydreamed* about housework? This is something I do most mornings. (smiles) I will sit in my chair near the hearth and think about how nice my house will look after I do the work. Most of the time, I actually put those daydreams into action and get results.

Other times, if I am weak or ill, I just walk away from what has to get done, and I keep daydreaming, and smiling. I know what my house will look like, or what I want it to look like, and that makes me happy. That gets me through those days when everything seems to pile up and all one can do is laugh!

So today, if you feel like you are surrounded by flooding water in your kitchen, with cups floating down the stairs, just smile and daydream about better housekeeping days!

An Unhurried Day

Wouldn't it be nice to have a quiet day? A day when we pretend there is no television, very little electricity, and no cars? I know that is not entirely practical, but maybe we can pretend for a few hours.

It would be nice to have a day of puttering around the property, working outdoors to make the grounds look nice, and to slowly tidy up the house. Maybe singing a few hymns while we work?

The day could start with Bible study and prayer. Then a little bit of housework. Perhaps the children are all still sleeping while we do these few things. We can be dressed and ready for the day with a cheerful smile, as if we have all the time in the world!

We can bake a special treat for the family, or just serve something special to surprise them for a mid-morning break.

Then perhaps we will go outside with them, and not say, "*I am too busy*." We can act like we are "retired" and have much leisure to just focus on family.

Will nothing distract us today? How sweet would that be?

Classic Old Fashioned Housewife

My husband's mother passed away at the beginning of this year. I have been thinking about her a lot. She was a true homemaker. She stayed home to care for the family and did not work. She kept her house neat and clean. I don't think I ever saw any clutter in her house. She raised six children and lived in a large Beach house in Massachusetts with her husband. She certainly had many hard times and financial troubles, but I have learned so much by just observing her daily life.

She would get up very early in the morning to make coffee. She would clean and cook and make things neat. Then she would sit at the kitchen table for a break. She took many breaks throughout the day. She would even visit with guests who came by. These were mostly her grown children.

I remember her looking out the window, into the yard, to watch her grandchildren play. She would smile and was so content. After that, she would go back to some household chore, do it cheerfully, and then go back to the window to watch the children.

We called her "Mem" (short for the French term for grandmother – "meme"). All her children adored her. The grandchildren loved her very much. She had a way of making each person feel special. Her entire life revolved around that house. *She had no outside care or responsibility.* Money was not an issue for her. If she had none, she went without. She did not complain or scheme to find a way to get some. She was content with whatever was provided for her.

Mem rarely left the property. She was the true Keeper at *Home*. Everyone knew exactly where her heart was. We knew home and family was everything.

This is the classic old fashioned housewife I have tried to be for all of my married life.

Sermons and the Godly Home

I have been listening to sermons this morning. They inspire, convict, encourage, exhort and help me stay on the right path, as a parent in a godly home. It is important to have a godly culture in the home.

This reminds me of something. Many years ago, when Nicole (now 21) was around 17 years old, we still owned a country store. She worked for us. It was a family business - Dad, Mom and all of our five children worked there. My parents even helped from time-to-time. But my job was mostly bookwork, inventory, finances, and occasional work behind the cash register helping the children.

Well, one night, Nicole came home from working her shift. She had been "in the world" with all kinds of customers she had to cater to, and wait on all day long. Well, she walked in the door to see me making a homemade supper. I had on my apron. I was happy. I was listening to hymns. I was smiling and setting the table. She walked in and just smiled. "Wow! This is a whole different world," she said. It was a different culture than what she just came from.

There should be a vast difference between the world and the culture of the home.

Since we are bombarded with humanistic thinking, worldly advertisements and an ungodly culture - listening to sermons on a regular basis -even daily if possible - will seriously help keep us focused on providing a precious, peaceful, holy environment where our children will *crave* and enjoy the hospitality and love of a godly home.

Rising While it is Yet Night

In Grandmother's day, homes were kept immaculate. There was a sense of pride in keeping a tidy, clean house. You would see freshly scrubbed pantry shelves, polished stoves, freshly washed floors, and spotless sinks. These capable homemakers worked hard and could be *trusted* to do their jobs right. This example helped train children to do their best at every task.

Mothers today can't seem to understand that it takes hard, difficult work to keep a home looking nice. Yes, we have times of sorrow, sickness, and babies who need us. But on *normal days*, we need to spend more time truly making a home. It must be sanitary, so the family stays healthy. Our dishes must be clean and put away. Our counters must be scrubbed and our floors must be washed.

The Virtuous woman rose while it was yet night and tended to her home duties. She was busy before the sun came up. Then she opened drapes and windows and greeted the silence of the early morning.

Before her family even woke up, she had her prayer time, her Bible study; she was dressed neatly, and had started breakfast. She is the ideal and what we, as godly homemakers, should strive for.

This morning, I am taking some extra time to clean and make things look nice. I have several errands to do and lots of activities that need my attention. But this morning, I woke up at 4 am and have been getting a head start on the day. I have been working slowly and happily. No one is underfoot. Everything is quiet. I will make sure everything is neat and pleasant and greet my family with a smile. There will be no rushing. Only a calm serenity.

The House Dress

My mother always wore a house dress at home. She would work, *or rest,* wearing a simple lounge dress or pretty nightgown. When it was time for church or shopping, she would get all dressed up. But once we were back home, the house dress was put back on.

My Mother-in-law (Meme) did the same thing. Whenever we visited her, she always had on a pretty nightgown. She would put her long hair up and she looked sweet and feminine, while she cooked and visited with us. I remember her standing by the window, watching all her grandchildren playing in the pool. She also puttered around the yard doing her gardening in one of her pretty house dresses.

It was common, in the old days, for homemakers to wear a simple dress in the home. This was a more durable dress, or something not quite fancy.

When I came home today, I put on my favorite summer nightgown. It is black with dainty pink polka dots and has capped sleeves. I put my hair up and I can do a little housework, then take a little break. I love being home and I love my House Dresses.

Let Us Not Be Weary

The Homemaker has one of the greatest jobs in the world. She is the keeper of the home and of the family. She creates beauty with her skills . . with her hands. . and with her heart.

In the early morning, she can be found in prayer and Bible study. Then she starts her daily tasks:

She does the mending, ironing and washing. She prepares the meals. She tends to the children. She helps her husband in his work. She is diligent, but takes many breaks for refreshment.

Obstacles come that seem insurmountable. Perhaps these are designed to force her to stop and remind her to rely on God, rather than on her own strength.

After a time of rest, she can continue on, creating beauty and joy for those around her.

In the evening hour, she settles her house down and soothes and *quiets* their weary souls. She comforts them with her kind compassion and she makes home the happiest place on earth.

Blue Collar – Working Class – Housewife

Sometimes I feel like a pampered housewife, *who has it made*. I don't have to earn money. I don't have to financially support my family. But I do have to work very hard at home.

In the old days, homemaking was more time consuming. Wash day was an enormous undertaking. Baking and Cooking, before processed foods were available, took the majority of mother's time.

Wealthier women could hire a cook, a maid and even a nanny to help with the children. These women were the pampered ones - they were the wealthy class. They did not have to work at all.

There is a middle ground - the white collar working class. I cannot speak for them, but I know they are well educated, work in specialized jobs - law, medicine, etc, and often hire help for some of the work at home.

As for the old fashioned, blue collar housewives, we are still here. There may not be as much heavy labor for us, but there is still so much to do! We must constantly economize, run errands, cook, clean, bake and care for our children. It is a struggle to come up with extra money for treats or presents. We have this healthy glow in our cheeks which comes from heavy labor.

Yesterday, I was reading "*Mama's Bank Account,*" by Kathryn Forbes. I love reading about life in the 1920's for the working class! This Immigrant Mama had such wisdom:

- Whenever she was relieved after a trial, or worry, she would say, "*Is Good.*" This comforted her family and herself.

- "A mop is never good. Floors should be scrubbed with a brush." [I loved this one!]

- I also loved how she would take the weekly income, sit at the table surrounded by her family, and carefully put coins in stacks for things like "The landlord," and "For the Grocer."

She was such a hardworking mother. She was a *working class* mother. These mothers have helped build this country with their own hands.

We mothers are still the foundation of society. Even though money is scarce, and we are often tempted to leave home to earn an income, our work at home . . . our *influence* at home, is **essential**.

An Old Fashioned House

I saw a picture of a lovely, old Victorian cottage. It was being sold in a nice area, here in Vermont. However, the price was so high, it made me sad. Why? Because it was packed with modern updates. There were stainless steel appliances, a "granite chef's kitchen," and "Quakermaid oak cabinets." But wait. . it gets worse. . . there is a "new Kohler bathroom." All these modern, high-end touches, make the price prohibitive for lower middle class families. If the house had just been left in its "old fashioned" state, with basic repairs, a little paint and some cleaning, it would have been absolutely charming! It would have been affordable to a low-income family, who would have been thrilled to own it.

People, in these days, forget that creativity and hard work are what make an inexpensive home lovely and valuable.

I remember watching a home- and- garden program. Viewers toured the home of an elderly woman who wanted to sell it. As the kitchen came into view, I saw the most beautiful cabinets I had ever seen! These were painted a sage color and the owner had stenciled delicate vines to make a subtle trim around the

For The Love of Christian Homemaking

edges. There were tiny hints of pale colored flowers. It looked lovely! However, the realtor advised the owner to replace those cabinets, saying that buyers today want modern, neutral fixtures. While that is generally true, something is being lost in our culture, when old fashioned houses are being replaced with modern, elegant features which are *only affordable* to dual-income career couples and the upper class.

Mr. White and I have a 3 story colonial house. It is 150 years old. We had some visitors come by in our first year here. They were retired, wealthy relatives. They looked around and said it would cost us a fortune to update this place. They shook their heads and said we had a lot of work to do. *I cannot comprehend that mind-set.* Why would I modernize this charming old house? Why would I not cherish it as the "museum" that it is? I love my large drafty rooms and my large, old windows. I love the old chimney and the homemade "Yankee" * kitchen cabinets. The charm of this house is that it is ***affordable***, lovely, and vintage. . . This is truly an old fashioned house. I can only hope that there are still many more out there.

* *The term "Yankee" implies New England ingenuity, by making do with what we have while using little or no money.*

The Romance of Home

Do you yearn for *home* when you are away? Is there a *homesickness* that makes you weary of the world? Our homes should be lovely and pleasant places. We should be the *creative force* behind the production of happy families.

So often, we mothers get tired and caught up in our troubles that we forget to remember the old days. When we were young, we longed for a home of our own. We longed for marriage and children. We romanticized a charming life in a grown up world. We were eager and ready to make the effort of happiness.

Now that the years have passed, it is time to re-evaluate our situation. I hear of so many people frustrated because life has gotten harder. Worries become burdens. Many watch the courtship and happiness of new young couples with a sadness - like they are missing out on something precious.

When Dad comes home from work, is he greeted with cheer? When the children come home from their play, or their jobs, are they happy to be there? When Mother has been out grocery shopping, does she drive in the driveway thankful to be back?

Here are a few ideas to help create an environment of a romantic home:

1. Have clean, fresh curtains in the living room - homemade, or lace, or whatever you like best.

I remember, in the old days, sitting in the car while my husband drove us up to his parent's home. There were beautiful, lace curtains in the kitchen window. They were charming. I have also seen lovely homemade curtains in some homes that just made things look so nice and well cared for. *This is part of romance - part of creating beauty.*

2. Keep a tidy kitchen, with a few simple decorative items.

We do the best we can to keep our kitchens looking nice. Food is so comforting. You hear of husbands and grown children talking about missing home-cooking and you know how important it is to have a kitchen which is ready for hospitality. If there are stacks of dishes, and no time to clean, just do what you can to make that mess look neater. Wipe down counters, sink, and stove. Sweep the floor. Have a few pretty things decorating the wall - even if it is artwork from the children. Just have something in that room to show that it is used and *loved. There is fondness in romance.*

3. Dress neatly and present yourself in a pleasant manner.

Keeping ourselves neat, even in casual clothes, sends a message that *we care.* We inspire those around us to want to be neat and pleasant. I remember when my girls were very little. If they did not get dressed and fix their hair in the morning, they were irritable and difficult, until they took the time to prepare for the day. *There is beauty in romance.*

4. In the evenings, try to have dim lights or candles with soothing, pleasant music playing softly.

This helps set a peaceful mood. It helps the family settle down. Sometimes, when mother has that gentle music playing and she smiles at her family, all the troubles and arguments seem to fade away. *There is serenity in romance.*

5. Avoid discussing problems and troubles other than at a set time.

I remember during my childhood. My Father would come home from work around 4 in the afternoon. We children stayed in the living room, or outside while Mother and Dad sat at the kitchen table to talk and visit. They discussed any troubles of the day, without any distraction or interference. When they were finished, we would happily visit with Dad and help Mom get the supper ready. The rest of the evening was happy and a time of contentment for us all. We felt secure and settled. *There is tranquility in romance.*

In order to have happy homes, we need to find ways of dealing with the trials of life. We need to create homes that our families will yearn for. We want them to be *wooed* back home, when they are away. We want them to *yearn* and *long - for* their romantic homes.

For The Love of Christian Homemaking

When Mother is Productive

Homemakers have such great opportunity to create their own work. They can keep busy with many projects and chores. I would rather make the extra effort to hang clothes on the line, rather than putting them in the dryer. I love the work and it keeps me productive.

I want my children to see me busy and happy. I want them to love the idea of working and find it satisfying.

It would be so easy for me to settle into a chair and spend all my time reading. Yes, the house would suffer, and I would get plenty of rest, but this is not a good example to my children.

I have noticed that if I am busy creating a sewing project, or decorating, or planning an adventure, the children seem to find plenty of their own projects. We become a productive family. No one is bored. Everyone is inventive.

We go to each other with our latest ideas with great eagerness and excitement. We are also available to each other as we work. There is time to chat while I sew. There is time to visit while the children draw or make a go-cart. We may even come up with ideas to earn some money from home. This creates an entrepreneurial spirit. It creates excitement!

I want my children to remember me busy and happy. I want them to know that "*Mother can do just about anything I need her to!*" I love that my grown children still call me for advice or to help them with an idea. They like to see that I have my own talents and abilities. Daily, I must cultivate those gifts.

The Basics of Home Life

What are the basics of home life?

1. Simple furniture.

2. Basic food, lovingly prepared and served.

3. Time spent reading to the Children in an unhurried fashion.

4. Clean and neat clothes for the family.

5. A Tidy, uncluttered Home (the ideal we must strive for).

6. Laughter and conversation.

7. Love.

8. A Warm welcome for all who enter.

Thoughts from Benjamin Franklin to encourage you in your housekeeping:

"If time be of all things the most precious, wasting time must be the greatest prodigality."

"Let us, then, be up and doing, and doing to the purpose. Sloth makes all things difficult, but industry all easy; and he that riseth late must not rest all day, and shall scarce overtake his business at the night, while laziness travels so slowly that poverty soon overtakes him."

"Work while it is called today; for you know not how much you may be hindered tomorrow."

"One today is worth two tomorrows; and never leave till tomorrow what you can do today."

"It is true there is much to be done, and perhaps you are weak handed; but stick to it steadily, and you will see great effects."

Baking Bread in the Quiet of the Morning

Everyone is sleeping. The House is dark and I am awake and ready for my quiet home duties. *I will do something special today*. I will make homemade bread. This is what the old housewives used to do. They would bake bread early in the morning.

I reserved some potato broth from supper the other night. I saved it in the fridge. I plan to use it as the liquid in my bread dough this morning. It will add a nice flavor.

First I will prepare the recipe from my old Betty Crocker Cookbook. I will stir and mix and then knead the dough by hand. I will do this while it is yet night. There is still darkness out my kitchen window. There is still peace and serenity.

I will work the dough while I say little prayers. Then as it is rising, I will wake up the house.

When everyone is up and getting ready for the day, I will visit with them and *smile* and listen to gospel music and I will prepare the dough for the second rising.

Then we will go out on an errand. *But the joy of the bread dough will call me back home.*

I will eagerly walk back into my kitchen, put on my apron and start shaping the loaves. Then I will start our homeschool.

When the dough is ready to bake, I will get that oven all warmed up, on this cold winter day, and then get back to our school work.

Soon the house will be filled with the aroma of freshly baked bread and we will all be filled with the warmth and love of home.

Pleasant Days by the Fire

I have great memories of resting by the fireside, this past winter. Early in the morning, I would do all my housework. Then I would look out the window and admire the snow covered landscape. I would sit in my favorite chair, near the hearth, and enjoy a warm fire. I had a cozy pillow and blanket and a small table beside me. I would read "*Dombey and Son*" by Charles Dickens. This 1000 page novel is a masterpiece. It took me months to read the entire book, because I wanted to savor each word. I would sit and read while sipping on hot chocolate with marshmallows. I did this during my homemaking breaks.

I would get up and prepare lunch and do more chores. Then it was time for another rest, near the fire, with my book. I would head back to my chair and enjoy a couple of pieces of *Freschetta* pizza. It was my favorite lunch! I would also sip on ginger-ale. I enjoyed that book so much and will re-read it again this coming winter.

This morning it is chilly here in Vermont. Mr. White just started up the wood stove. I am contemplating reading a book for the spring. Perhaps it will be another Dickens classic. Or maybe I will start with Austen. Whatever the novel is, I am sure it will be delightful. But I dearly look forward to the next winter, when I can sit by the fire, and enjoy my favorite chair and my special breaks.

Trials and Grandmother's Rocking Chair

I have an old rocking chair which belonged to my grandmother. She was from Alabama and was married to a preacher. She had many trials in her life. She was a dear lady. I have decided to bring that rocking chair into my living room as a reminder of my grandmother. I will sit and rock, when times get rough, and sing her favorite hymn, *"Tempted and tried . . . we'll understand it all by and by."*

When a trial happens, the best thing to do is just start working. Just start cleaning or fixing supper. Say prayers and let the tears fall, but get some housework done. This will help bring peace.

We can think of the generations before us, and the hard work they accomplished at home each day. Our grandmothers read their Bibles and went to church and prayed. They had great wisdom. Yet our culture is changing and we often feel like pioneers in a new world and don't know how to handle anything. Remembering the history of our families and the old days will help us keep our bearings.

This afternoon, I am going to bring out the old rocking chair and I am going to sit quietly and pray and sing some of the old hymns and remember my heritage.

Take Back the Home

Children can give us trouble. Teenagers can drive us crazy. And husbands can sometimes be difficult to bear. Mothers have so much to face each day that it can be overwhelming. She may want to cower off somewhere and wait for the next "shoe to drop" before she gives up entirely. Or she may even play with the idea of moving out on her own (running away)! When these rough times come, this is when her courage is most needed. This is when her creativity must come into play.

Mother must stand strong and **Take Back The Home**!

Many horrible things happened to me the last few days. I was devastated by my circumstances and felt powerless to change them. But I finally realized that this is MY home. I am in charge. I am the mistress of this castle and it will be run in a *rated G way*! (smiles) It is to be a godly home. It is to be a wholesome home. Worldly troubles are not allowed indoors. Rule-breakers will be firmly told not to step over the line, or consequences will keep coming, no matter how weary this mother gets. I decided to take back my home.

First I put on my very favorite Edwardian apron. I wore my prettiest clothes and even a pearl necklace. My mood and my courage require an appropriate uniform to show my authority as the Mother and Housewife of this lovely place.

Next, I turned on my kitchen radio to hear a sermon of my late Uncle, a preacher from rural Alabama. (He passed away in 1995, but many of his sermons had been recorded.) As I listened, I remembered my childhood visits to his country church and the beauty of precious holiness, and godly living. My courage began to soar. I cleaned and made our humble house look lovely.

I set out a game of chess on the parlour table. Teenagers came by and spent *hours* happily playing together. They were peacefully occupied!

A certain teenager stopped listening to her worldly music. Another began to clean up his messes. The children started to smile and laugh and to, *once again*, bring joy to our hearts. A grumpy husband cheered up because his wife was suddenly happy again, and devoted to home.

After I spent the morning cleaning and loving my housework, I sat in a parlour chair to rest. Mr. White walked by and smiled at me. He said he was very grateful to have me for his wife.

I had taken back my home.

A Cold House on a Winter Day

In our old colonial house, we have a wood pellet stove. It broke a few nights ago. Mr. White ordered a replacement part and it should arrive any day. In the meantime, I am thinking about how to keep this home a cozy, inviting place despite the forlorn cold. When we walk in the door from errands, we sense an emptiness. There is nothing like a warm fire on a winter day, to gladden the heart. We all miss it.

This morning, it is snowing heavily. I plugged in a portable electric heater to bring us a little warmth. It is in our parlour and should help take off some of the chill. This 14 room house has multiple sources of heat. On the third floor suite, it is always warm. On part of the first floor is where my parents live. They have a real old fashioned wood stove that doesn't break. We can visit with them at any time for some hot chocolate, to hear stories, and to enjoy the cozy stove.

But I love being in my own section of the house - my parlour and my kitchen. I love to clean and tidy and cook and bake. I enjoy listening to old gospel music by J. D. Sumner and The

Kingsmen Quartet, while I work. I love to sit in my favorite chair, near the window and enjoy my homemaking breaks.

Right now, I am thinking about Ma Ingalls and how she made her home inviting. The family often battled cold and found ways to bring happiness. Perhaps I will get my yarn and do a little crocheting this morning. I can light a candle on the table to bring the impression of a fire and some warmth. I will also do a little cleaning and bake some brownies.

Tomorrow is Thanksgiving. All my children will come home. I will gather them around our electric heater and serve hot chocolate. Our stories and laughter will warm up the room and create a pleasant memory, while we wait for that stove part to arrive.

The Sweet Voice in the Kitchen

I must have been very ill today. I *slept away* most of the day. I remember cleaning my kitchen this morning and smiling while I worked. Then I laid down for a few minutes to rest. . . I fell asleep for hours. . .

I have teenagers here at home and everyone had projects of their own. They didn't seem to mind that Mother was sleeping. It made for a quiet day.

But the strange part was, when I finally got up to start working again, it was 4 in the afternoon. I put the laundry on the clothesline, hoping for the last bit of warmth from the sun. I could not believe how tired I had been.

I went into the kitchen and did some dishes. I was weak and weary and could not move at my usual pace.

Then I heard a voice. . .

It was my 13 year old son, John. "*Mom, can I do those dishes for you?*"

I loved cleaning, but knew I should accept his offer. I continued to work, but said I would love his help.

He *urged* me to go back to bed. He would make me a little supper and some hot chocolate.

I was grateful.

I laid back down and watched an episode of *"The Waltons"* while I enjoyed some food. The house was very peaceful. I thought about how much I wanted to just sit and read the Bible. It is amazing how *weariness* and *helplessness* can draw us closer to God. It also amazes me how sweet my children can be to me when I am somber and quiet. If only I was that good all the time.

Missing Church on Sunday

I love Sunday mornings. I love that we are all dressed up and ready to go worship the Lord together at Church. I love the sight of my family walking into the building, holding Bibles.

But, sadly, today I must stay at home. I have been worn out this past week and I have to miss church.

Since I will be at home. . .

1. I will look through my hymn book and read the songs.

2. I will watch Charles Stanley on Inspiration television.

3. I will do only minimal housework.

4. I will read from the Psalms - perhaps all of chapter 119.

Very often, Grandpa and Nana (who live with us) have health issues and aren't able to attend church. On those days, I can hear the sound of an old country preacher coming up through the house. Grandpa has cassette tapes of sermons from the old south, including the sermons of his late brother, who was an amazing preacher.

I also hear old gospel music throughout the house. Those are the *happiest*, most *comforting* sounds of all. Hearing Preachers and Gospel music, to me, are *the sounds of home* - whether it is Sunday or any other day of the week.

The Neglected Garden

I went to my mother's porch a few days ago. I walked along, looking at all her plants. She had so many colorful flower boxes, sitting on top of the railing. There was also a large tomato plant on the floor. She had all kinds of flowers growing in different planters.

As I walked, I realized the great *neglect*. Mother is away and asked me to take care of her plants. I had agreed to water them - to visit them. I had planned to go out there each day and tend to her beautiful *porch garden*. But on the first day, it rained. On the second day, it rained again. I didn't think the flowers needed me. So I stayed indoors. By the end of the week, I suddenly realized I needed to check on them. But it was too late.

The flowers were dying. They had been abandoned. They were forlorn and pitiful because of my careless neglect.

I quickly found a watering can and tried to revive them. For two straight days, I diligently tended them. They are showing no progress.

This reminds me of my home. It can be tempting to ignore all the work I have to do. It is easy to just put it off . . . But this will lead to a forlorn place. . . It will not look like a lovely garden. Weeds will spring forth. Flowers will wilt. Doom and gloom will be the aura of an abandoned home. It would be a sad place indeed, if I neglect my home, the way I neglected Mother's garden.

Inspiration for Home Life

I was reading the autobiography of Patricia St. John. A portion of the book is a tribute to her father. She described the beauty of a Christian Home. Some of what she said about her father:

"He never spoke a discourteous word about anybody and we never heard an impatient or unloving word between him and our mother."

"He encouraged us to enjoy ourselves and he loved to give us treats; but we knew he denied himself and kept his body under strict discipline; and the positive, radiant holiness that went on its own way, seldom criticizing or scolding, was extraordinarily constructive and controlling."

"So we grew up and he watched and waited never trying to force upon us the spiritual riches he had stored up for us until we were ready."

"He emphasized the importance of *example*, quoting John Bunyan's words, 'I was very careful to give my children no occasion to blame, lest they should not be willing to go on pilgrimage.' "

Patricia was a dedicated missionary, who wrote several books. I delight in reading about her adventures, her wisdom and the miracles she witnessed throughout her life. I am inspired by her victories, despite times of misery all around her. Surely her parents were a tremendous influence who helped her, *by their living testimonies*, become who she was.

A Lovely Rainy Night

It is quiet and peaceful here at home. The sky is dark. The evening hour has come. Rain is pouring on the roof. It is a pleasant sound.

Earlier today, I left the clothes on the line. *But I didn't care.* I love to see laundry on the line, even if a sudden rain drenches them!

Many years ago, Mr. White and I were house hunting here in rural Vermont. We were going to buy an old farmhouse. It had been owned, for a lifetime, by one family. In this house, things were still run like in the old days. There was a cookstove in the kitchen. We thought it was charming. There were no showers - only a claw foot tub. But the most endearing thing of all, was the rows- and- rows of clothes-lines, hanging on the covered porch. We were told that, *even in the dead of winter*, farm wives would hang the clothes outdoors! Later, they brought them in, *stiff*, and ready for a hot iron.

As the rain falls on this warm summer night, I am thinking about the old ways of housekeeping. I love the labor involved in keeping things neat. I love that I have important things to do, here at home.

I am also very grateful, that we bought this large old colonial house instead of the farm house. Because, honestly, I dearly love the idea that we live in a house that was built for a lawyer, who had a wife and 10 children. I love that this house is my museum. And I love the retreat-like-setting we get to enjoy, even though this place is beat -up, and in need of repairs.

There is nothing like a little rain, to make one nostalgic.

A Clean and Happy Home

I have been working on my kitchen for the past hour. The dark green counters are polished and clean. The sage cabinets, red breadbox, and pretty curtains make the room look very unique. I love to keep it clean.

A few months ago, I ran out of kitchen matches. I really miss lighting candles. I usually keep a large scented one on the center of my stove top. I am missing that little touch of romance in my home.

I gave the children a list of chores to accomplish by 3 p.m. It has been lovely seeing them help with the household tasks.

In just a little while, I will start supper. But first, I want to straighten pillows in the parlour. I want to vacuum the carpet and tidy the hutch shelves. I want to dust the window sills.

I will listen to Mozart, on my kitchen radio, while I work. There is nothing like the joy of a clean and happy home.

Settling in to a Simpler Life at Home

I have been working on making life simpler for my family. I want less pressure. I want less stress. The only way I can do this is if I have very few obligations.

I need time for unhurried family life.

I need to have all the time in the world to hear stories and ideas from my growing children.

I need to be found in the *same old places* by my children - the kitchen or parlour. I want them to have that security of knowing where to find me.

I need to be able to cook and bake and serve my family without fear of deadlines.

I want peace and happiness that comes from a surrendered Christian witness.

The greatest thing I can do, is to simply be a *wife* and *mother* **here at home**.

The Dinner Hour

I entered my parlour this afternoon, after being out in the cold on errands. We had *bags* and *papers* and *things* everywhere. It was time to prepare (mentally and literally) for the dinner hour.

I turned on a sermon tape, on my kitchen radio, of A. W. Tozer, "*The Plague of the Heart,*" and worked in my home, while being nourished and strengthened by godly wisdom.

Soon the dishes, from the day, were soaking. The counters looked neat. The table was cleared and shining. The chairs were in order and the floor was picked up. *Home looked lovely.*

I will light a candle before the sun sets. I will get the Bibles ready to prepare for evening worship, after dinner. There will be no watching of television, or computer time, or listening to secular news or music. It will be a sacred time of our family gathering together at our family table. *It will be the dinner hour.*

To make the dinner hour successful takes labor, and vision, and an eagerness to enjoy home. *It takes a pushing aside of all worldly thoughts and worries and activities.* It is time to calm the heart and to soothe the soul. It is time to make *family* and *loveliness* and *charm* and *the beauty of home* a sacred obligation.

We will pray and eat and enjoy fellowship at the family table. It will be a precious time because Mama made it happen.

The Long Awaited Present

One day last year, my daughter Nicole (23) called me from the city where she lives. A book store was going out of business and she had bought me a little treasure. It was "*The Prize Winner of Defiance.*" We had both seen the movie a few times and loved it. But to read the actual book, with so many more details, and much more to learn from, would be wonderful!

I waited for her to mail me the book. She lived too far away for me to visit very often, so mailing a package seemed the only way. Months went by and no sign of the book. We both visited each other and forgot about it.

Then one day this week, I was in the city helping her move when I came across the book in a pile on the windowsill. *"My book?"* I smiled at her. She nodded. I shoved it into my purse and we quickly finished our work and headed out.

Back at home, these last few days, during my homemaking breaks, I have been sitting on parlour chairs, propped up in bed, or on the front porch and reading the little treasure. It is a memoir by Terry Ryan about her mother who had 10 children. They lived in dire straits, with an alcoholic father, but the mother was ingenious and courageous. I love the time period (1950's), the community, the values, the trivia about the church and all the little remembrances of such a childhood and family. It fascinates me that the mother didn't know how to drive! I love that many mothers were home more than we are today.

I will share two passages with you I just read this morning:

1. After walking to the police station to pick up her teenage son who had gotten into a little trouble:

"It's pretty discouraging, Rog. I've spent most of my life trying to raise a bunch of kids under some pretty trying circumstances, only to see you do something as stupid as this."

2. This glimpse of the times is incredible -

"Mom gave birth every two years or so, not that there was any system to it - birth control wasn't even discussed in Catholic households in the 1940's and 1950's."

The book includes the Mother's routine, as a writer, who entered an enormous amount of contests sponsored by companies like "Dial soap," and "Quaker oats." These are entertaining and I loved the description of her ironing while she wrote, or sitting in the living room with the children and sharing her ideas with them. Her many wins are incredible!

But the most endearing thing for me, is reading about her daily struggles, her humor and her life as a blessed mother of many children. Reading this book, during my breaks here at home, has given me a surge of inspiration, which has been greatly needed!

The Basics of Lovely Housekeeping

Some days it doesn't take very long to tidy up my house. The kitchen is quickly cleaned, the parlour is neat, the laundry is in the machine and the floors are swept. Once everything is in order, I sometimes wonder, "*Have I done enough?*" or "*Is it possible that I can go do some other pleasant thing?*" Those are the lovely moments of doing basic housekeeping.

Yesterday, I was reading from "*Great Expectations.*" One of my girls found a beautiful hardcover copy of this at Marshalls the last time we were in the city. I was delighted when she bought it for me. The rich literary wit and historical insights are amazing. I found myself taking the book into other rooms in the house to share interesting passages with the children. Next, I took an early afternoon rest by watching an old Frank Sinatra movie. But one can only take so much of worldly amusements, so I turned on the gospel music and did some more housework.

Even though the day was slow paced and pleasant, I was still busy with the grandbaby, my teenagers and errands. The housework seemed to take care of itself, in very quick bursts of cleaning. I had much leisure time and was delighted.

When a child gets ready to do some home chore, he is often overwhelmed. He may procrastinate and take hours on a job that really only takes minutes. This is what makes housework seem tedious, boring and painful. When we mothers go in with a cheerful attitude and a spring in our step, we can make very basic housework look delightful. We can accomplish a lot in a short time and then be free for other things.

One of my girls is like that. She will go into a room, tidy up a mess in minutes and come back like she didn't exert herself in any way. The bright happy look in her eyes and the pleasant proud smile delight our home. She can make the house look so pretty with very little effort.

If we just realized that basic housework is only sweeping, cooking, washing, laundry and other such minor tasks, we would enjoy much more time of looking about the room, sighing content and sitting to rest in a happy, clean home.

Truly, Housekeeping is a lovely occupation.

A Pink Day

Have you ever looked around your house and thought it was all just *overwhelming*? I don't mean that it was so beautiful and clean that you were in awe. . . (smiles). . I mean that you were the only creative force, in charge of all the work it takes to make a pleasant home.

We run errands, we care for our families, we do chores. We are tired. Sometimes we need to motivate ourselves by saying something like, "*I am going to have a Pink Day*!" This means everything around me will be made lovely.

Today, I am going to get to work and make it happen. I am going to be cheerful, smiling, laughing and happy.

I will get dressed up and be the *hostess of our home*. There will be a "dinner party" at 5 p.m. I will set the table with our prettiest dishes. And even if the dinner bounty consists of take-out, or heated frozen dinners, I know I have done my best to make this a happy place to be!

Comforted by my Homemaking Tools

I have this old ironing board that I have used for many years. It is wobbly and the cover is faded and worn. I did some ironing yesterday. I set it up in front of the television and watched "The Waltons" while I ironed pillowcases and fabric for sewing projects. I took breaks from ironing to wash bed sheets and make beds. I did dishes, made lunch and enjoyed a very special homemaking day.

I love the scent of a hot iron, and the feel of warm clothes. It reminds me of the comfort of home. When it was time to put the ironing board away, I thought of how it would be nice to get a new one. But then realized I needed to keep this old one. It has been well-used, all these years, and is an important part of my life. Why would I replace it with something *modern* and *cold* and *foreign*? I need to be surrounded by the familiar. I need to look at my homemaking tools and remember they have been used year-after- year and that I've done well.

One thing that is difficult about using a computer is that it is very hard to keep house while surfing the Internet or checking emails, or writing. But when I watch television or listen to the radio, I can iron and sew and walk about the house doing projects. I can dust and polish and visit with my family. I can interact with those around me and accomplish things that give me great joy.

I mostly try to use the computer in the very early hours before sunrise. Then I spend the rest of my day focusing on the joy of the home arts - familiar things - surrounded by my family - and ironing and sewing and doing dishes. Even the mere act of sweeping the floor provides a good feeling. I love to see the vacuum cleaner and the broom and my dustpan, over in the corner. I see the furniture polish under the kitchen shelf, and my sewing basket on the hutch, and I know these special tools are part of my daily life. It is a rich and full life. *I am ever-grateful.*

For The Love of Christian Homemaking

Who Will Help Mother?

I cannot tell you how many times I've asked my children to help me with my projects and my chores. When they were little, they were delighted. But when they got older, they had their own projects, activities and agendas. This is something I have to constantly remind myself - the importance of enjoying my daily duties.

While children should certainly have their own chores, Mother needs to have her own work as well. Have you ever watched Ma Ingalls on "Little House on the Prairie?" Mary and Laura were busy with school. They also had homework in the evenings. But they had specific tasks to do at home - *and then they were done*! Mother didn't try to slave-drive them all day long. No, she did her *own* work, just like Pa did his.

If I am busy in the kitchen, or working in the living room, or doing laundry, there is often a teenager nearby talking to me about his day. If I said to my teens, "*Hey, can you help me with that*?" Don't you think they'd find something else to do, and fast? (smiles) It's not that they don't want to help me, but they want to see Mother busy with her own responsibilities. They don't want to think that Mother is always trying to get out of her chores. It sets a bad example. They want to see Mother diligent and content with her daily agenda.

Yesterday, I cleaned and baked. I had plenty of time for leisure. I read for a while, did some writing, and then did the laundry. I did not ask anyone the age-old, weary question, "*Will someone please help me??*"

But if I were sick, or not able-bodied, the family would certainly step in and do my work for me. If I had a baby, or a toddler who needed most of my time, the family chores would fall more heavily on the rest of the family, so I could be free to care for the younger ones. But when Mother doesn't have those kinds of things going on, she would do well to get into the habit of learning to love her own work and be about her own household business.

Creating a Cozy Home

My biggest goal this year is to get rid of everything I don't use or need. I want my home to feel like a relaxing place to be. I have thousands of books in my home library and am in the process of donating many of them to our local library. I also have 20 years worth of school books and curriculum I am ready to part with. Do I want to sell them? No. I would rather just donate them all at once.

I have closets full of clothes and shoes I don't need. I want to eliminate and simplify this all down to the basic necessities and then add in some charming pretty items.

I would love to have our parlour painted a pretty country blue. I want fresh flowers in vases. I want polished windows and furniture. I want pretty plants and beautiful paintings on the walls. This will be our *welcome room*. I remember reading this old book recently. A gentleman came to the door of a small country estate. A servant opened the door. She invited him in, saying "Come in, the parlour was just cleaned." In other words, it was ready for guests. In our house, the parlour is the living room. It is the first room a guest sees when they enter our home.

All this work of creating a cozy home is how I get ready for a wonderful spring! I will have an enormous head start before spring cleaning time arrives. My house will have only the *basics* and the *treasures*. All else will be donated and removed from our estate. This will help eliminate wasted time in searching for things, or all the extra cleaning, and help me enjoy the coming seasons.

I have every intention of sewing this spring, and hanging clothes on the line. I plan to spend much of my time outdoors creating a lovely garden, even though I know nothing about landscaping! But the fun. . . and the delight . . . in working outdoors and making this place beautiful *in my own humble, simple way* will give me great joy!

Afternoon Tea Break

It is so cold and snowy here in Vermont that my car wouldn't start this morning. I was not able to do any of my necessary errands. Yet, the reaction from my family, when I told them to cancel *work* and *classes* and *plans*, was relief and delight!

I am grateful for a pantry full of food. I spent the morning cleaning and baking while listening to "Crooners" which is the title given to singers in the 1940's. I listened to Perry Como, Bing Crosby and more. It makes cleaning house nostalgic and peaceful.

Last night, it was terribly dark in the kitchen because of our broken light. It seemed like the nightlight and candle were not enough for me while I worked. Amy (16) suggested I put a small lamp on the kitchen counter. I was delighted with this suggestion and couldn't believe I had not thought of it myself. We now have this pretty lamp, complete with a delicate little lampshade sitting near my canisters. The kitchen looks dreamy in the evenings.

I am just about to cuddle up near the hearth with some tea and enjoy a freshly baked muffin. I will read a nice book and be *pleasant*.

Struggling to Keep House

I just finished reading a few chapters in the Bible. It is getting late, but I want to do a little housework. I have been in pain all day and resting. . . *I miss cleaning.* I miss the work of making a home. . .

Sometimes, when I am in too much pain, I think about taking Tylenol, just to make the pain stop so I can have a normal life. But I don't. I would rather rest and avoid the medicine. After a few days, it always goes away. It gets better.

I will try to rest more often so I am not on my feet too much. That is when the pain comes. I can only do so much before I wear out.

I am sure I will be fine by tomorrow, but I just don't like missing out on homekeeping. It is a quiet, reflective art - *to make and keep a home.*

I think I will turn on some soothing Classical music and tidy up for a little while. Then I can rest, content and happy.

Tomorrow will be a better day.

The Sewing Hour

There is a time, in a homemaker's day, called *The Sewing Hour*. It is when she sits quietly in the parlor and works on the sewing. Perhaps she is mending the family wardrobe? Or maybe she is hand-sewing a hem on a new garment? I am often working on an apron. There was a time when I would crochet a baby afghan, or sew a toddler quilt while praying or singing hymns. This is a precious time of quiet devotion.

I urge you, dear ones, to use this time to listen to a godly, inspiring, *convicting* sermon.

When the hour has past, you will put down your sewing and your heart will be full. Even though you may hold back tears (because of the sermon), you will *get up and minister to your family!*

Mother Makes the Home

We live in a secular culture. We are bombarded by images, attitudes and values that are decayed and destructive. Yet, our homes do not have to be that way. The presence of a godly Mother can make home a precious place for her family.

Despite what goes on in the world, Mother can be about the Master's business at home. It should be a peaceful place where love and mercy abound. She will go about her daily duties after a time of prayer and private Bible study. She needs the spiritual strength.

She will clean and bake and cook. She will listen to her children's woes and give them guidance. She will show them love by her actions and words. She will be the anchor of the family.

At times there will be trials and annoyances within the family. But these soon pass if we are patient and long-suffering. We forgive quickly and try to keep each other cheered up.

It is amazing how teenagers will choose worldly music over sermons or gospel. They would rather sing the catchy tunes of society, rather than the old church hymns. That is why Mother will take the initiative and keep a godly culture in the home.

Perhaps, at times, she is tempted to listen to the worldly music. But then, just for a moment, she forgets the eternal goal for her family. When she makes the effort to turn on a sermon- CD or sing a hymn from the old hymnbook, she is far more blessed and rewarded for her efforts than she ever thought imaginable.

Mother is the conductor. She is a guide, director, mentor; the mistress of the home. She will gather the children around for Bible time. Some may respond eagerly. Others may sigh with annoyance. Nevertheless, in years to come, they will never forget that *Mother made the home.*

When Mama is an Invalid

I have struggled with chronic illness for many years. In 1997, I was diagnosed with cancer and have not been the same since. However, I have many months of seeming perfect health, but then I have periods of total weakness and feeling like an invalid. There are times when I cannot walk and need crutches to support myself.

Most of the time, I "take it" cheerfully. It is like a forced break from all the things I try to do. It is time to sit quietly and enjoy some rest. Yet, I will do it with grace and glamor!

I love to watch old programs like "The Donna Reed Show." In her day, women kept up their looks even when ill. This morning, I swept my hair up, into a French twist, put on some extra makeup (like the 60's look), and have on my pretty red house-robe. I will rest in style.

I plan to give the children lists of housework to do for me. Someone will take charge of the kitchen. Another will take over laundry. I will also have one of them plan a special supper. If I see them keeping up the house, I will be able to rest content.

My grandmother had multiple sclerosis and, for as long as I can remember, lived in her wheelchair. She also lived with us from the time I was 3 years old until she died when I was 11. She was wonderful! She directed and managed the house, and everyone, from her chair. She had dignity and spunk and knew how to run a house. She also continued to do whatever work she could from that wheelchair. She is my inspiration.

If I am to be an invalid, I will still have a lovely home. I will manage from my chair and I will be *grateful* even in this trial.

No Matter What it Cost Me

When we first moved to Vermont from Massachusetts, I had just gotten out of the hospital for severe physical problems. I had been a cancer patient years before and was undergoing tests and treatment for more difficulties. It was unbearable and I continued to suffer.

When we arrived in Vermont, to our newly purchased country store, Mr. White and I had a deal. I would help him, along with our children, for one year, then he would hire an employee to take over so I could tend to our home cares. This proved to be the most difficult year of my entire life. I am grateful I was right there with my husband and children. We lived *above* the store and it was like one big house. But most nights, I would fall into bed in tears of agony. My frail body could not endure the trauma of so much work for very long. Or, so I thought...

After many months of this, I suddenly began to heal. Most of my pain was gone. I had become stronger. I had worked so hard and the Lord had rewarded me with better health. I did my duty, no matter what it cost me.

I thought about this last night. I have been ill for several days. Just so weary. I was tempted to skip my Bible study. I was just about to fall asleep when I remembered something from the book, *"Stepping Heavenward,"* by Elizabeth Prentiss. You see, the main character, Katy, was staying up late waiting for her husband to come home. In the room with her was her elderly father-in-law who had just arrived that day to live with them. He was depressed and sorrowful. His wife had died and he felt like a burden. But he said something significant. He said something like: "At what hour does my son do family prayers?" It was getting very late at night, and he dearly needed sleep. Katy told him not to worry, but to go on to bed. There was no need to wait for his son to come home. But he responded with something like this - **"I will do my duty, no matter what it cost."**

When I remembered this passage from the book, I was stung in the heart with conviction. I was startled out of my selfish stupor of being tired, and called for my Bible and record book. My dear son John (13) fetched them for me and we sat down together and did our Bible time. We did this no matter how tired we were, or how sick I was. We did it no matter what it cost.

The Smiling Mask of Mother's Pain

We mothers deal with so much trauma. It is in our homes, in our world, and in our minds. Right now I am suffering massively with physical ailments. Last Sunday, I woke up and tried so hard to go to church. I actually drove partway and realized I couldn't make it. I went back home and back to bed. I stayed there, off and on for 3 days. . . I have not recovered. . . It is a *weary* sort of sickness. It is not something that is contagious or that can be diagnosed. But it is disabling.

I am trying to smile and make light of it. One minute I am up and writing, or trying to clean something, the next I am sound asleep. It is a puzzle to the children. My step has slowed. My work is neglected.

But I am smiling, with that sort of *saint-like* nature that means I am helpless and grateful.

Our children deal with so much in the world. They have problems to contend with in their own lives. They need the comfort of mother's smiles.

We need to do our very best to hide our pain. We need to make home a place of rainbows and cheer, even if we cannot walk very fast, or clean as well as we would like. We must not complain or let despair overcome us.

The children know we suffer. They live with us. They see enough of it. Our job is to encourage their innocence, and enjoy their daily antics.

If we can endure to the end, *with that gentle, smiling mask,* what a sweet memory that will be, of their dear mother.

Getting Ready To Face the Family

Today, are you getting ready to face your family? Will they be comforted by your loving presence? Will their morning grumpiness fade away in the shadow of your cheerfulness?

This morning, I listened to one of my favorite songs, "Without Him." It was from the Gospel Hour on Youtube. They were paying tribute to 90 year old Eva Mae LeFevre. She got married at 17 and lived a godly life. She was an old-time gospel singer with her family. In this tribute, her son Mylon, in his 60's, said he was proud to be her son. He told her, "You're a wonderful godly Mother."

She died in 2009, less than 2 years after this tribute was recorded. Eva was a classy, kind lady. And I want to be just like her.

After watching this program, and getting my heart in order, I am ready to face my family this morning.

For The Love of Christian Homemaking

Reading the Bible in the Parlour

I sit in one of the chairs during my homemaking breaks. I read, or gaze out the window at the snowy landscape. Sometimes I do a little hand-sewing. Throughout the day, children will come and sit with me. We visit and laugh and share stories. When my husband comes home from work, we all gather there and talk and enjoy family time.

Last night, I was alone in the warm parlour. I saw my hymn book and wanted to sing. I called John (13) to join me. We did our Bible time. He read a Psalm to me. Then we sang a hymn and prayed. We were both so happy. Matthew (17) walked by. He was on the phone. He heard us singing. He stopped and listened. He smiled.

The parlour is a room for company. There is no television. There is no computer. It is a special room for visiting. There may be a table for games. There are plenty of cozy chairs. There might also be a bookcase full of great literature. Any room can be made into a parlour. It is so nice in there, even with humble furniture, one will want to read the Bible and be happily content.

Putting the House in Order

I have been working on domestic duties the last few days. I feel like an old housewife. This home is enormous and is hard to keep up with. Slowly, each day, I try to do a little, then take a break. Then I do a little more, and rest again. I love this way of life, but am making no progress. I think I will do a weekly tossing of things that are cluttering up the house.

Wouldn't it be delightful to have domestic servants? I would want a butler to answer the door and the phone. I would like a gardener to handle the property all year round. I would like a maid and a cook. I want them to help me with my work. I would not want them to do *everything* for me. I just want the help. But they must be capable and hard working. They also must have kindness and dignity, and loyal hearts.

At this moment, I have some dishes soaking in the sink. I will wash down the counters and sweep the floor. Then I will sit and read for a bit. I also have some laundry and meal planning to attend to. Last night, I baked some brownies. I set aside a few and wrapped them up and placed them in a special decorative box. Mr. White will be visiting an elderly neighbor soon. He will bring the package as a little "visiting" gift. Don't you love it when someone stops by unexpectedly and brings you a special treat?

I have to say, my greatest goal in life is to Stay Home. This place will never be bereft of domestic supervision. A homemaker is a mistress of her estate. It is an honor.

Morning Devotions for the Family

Before the invention of television, video games, and radios, families had more time for religious duties. We often get caught up in doing *good things*. Yet, sometimes those good things are *overindulged,* instead of done in moderation.

One of the most important things we can do, with our families, is have a time of morning devotions. We can gather around the living room, or kitchen table. Everyone comes with a sense of awe and reverence - it is family devotion. The Bible is read by Dad. The Mother smiles warmly at her children. The little ones and teens sit quietly and listen closely. Then it is prayer time and the family is dismissed to the events of the day.

What a precious way to begin the morning.

Family Worship increases the spirit of reverence for God and His Word. Children copy their parents' spirit and example. If parents begin the day by invoking God's blessing, by consecrating the early hour to His service, they show their estimate of the value of worship. - Rev. M. Simpson

Old Fashioned Home

In the old days, Mothers were always at home. The children felt safe and well taken care of. Mothers worked hard with cooking and baking and housekeeping. They were skilled and capable. Yet, there was an amazing amount of love in an old fashioned home.

Mother would guide her children throughout the day - in manners, kindness, chores, and the Bible. She would pray with her babies and she would read them stories in an unhurried way.

She baked cookies and made hearty meals to nourish and comfort her loved ones. She could be seen in an apron and a house dress. When it was time for Church or to head into town, Mother would get all dressed up, looking her best. The children were in awe of her.

Her entire life revolved around her family and creating a home-culture of godliness. Worldly thoughts or materialism were the furthest things from her mind. She lived on the strictest economy and was a good steward of the money and things she was provided with.

Mother was wise in heavenly matters. She labored each day with eternity in mind. Not only for herself, but with the decisions she made for her children and household. Some of the children would balk at her. They were young and wanted to have some worldly fun. But later on, as they looked back, they realized Mother was steadfast and strong in her beliefs and would not bend with the whims of society. They were drawn to the peace and faith of their dear mother.

Domestic Occupations

My Mother could set up a home anywhere. She would just start setting up a kitchen and living room. Then she would set up the bedrooms. She can do this, seemingly, out of nothing. She has a tremendous love for homemaking and cleaning. I believe this has a lot to do with the basic foundation of housewifery.

There are daily tasks that must be accomplished. These are *domestic occupations*, and include:

1. Dishes.

2. Laundry.

3. Sweeping.

4. Washings counters, floors, sinks.

5. Dusting.

6. Making beds, putting away clothes.

7. Preparing Meals.

8. Setting up tables and chairs for the comfort of the family.

The heart of these occupations stems from a deep love of hospitality and wanting the family to be happy and comfortable. It is a *servant's heart.* If the housewife has the basic knowledge and heart for these tasks, she can make a beautiful home anywhere she lives.

The Parlour in the Morning

It is early in the morning and the sun has not yet come up. It is dark and lovely in our cozy house. A few minutes ago, I walked into the parlour and saw the blazing wood stove and a calming gentle light casting shadows in the little room. I saw my favorite chair and wanted nothing more than to sit and read and get warm before anyone woke up. I will do that in just a little while.

I will make a little hot chocolate in a pretty tea cup. Then I will settle myself down and enjoy the quiet. A few days ago, I finished reading *"Dombey and Son"* by Charles Dickens. It was a sad and precious story. Now I am working on a new book. It is set in early America when most households had servants. It is intriguing and entertaining. But best of all, it is a Christian book by Revell.

All too soon, the family will be awake and wanting breakfast and conversation. The house will come to life and it will be pleasant. I will be delighted to face the family with happiness and cheer. But first, I must sit in the dimly lit, cozy parlour and read my book and drink hot chocolate.

Their Memories of Home

While I was in the kitchen tonight, making homemade beef stew, I watched the sun set out the front window. I turned on a lamp and tidied up. I stirred the food and then turned on some old gospel music. This is the kind of music my father listened to in the house, while we children were growing up. I kept playing one song over and over again, "*Without Him,*" because there is a portion of the song, where the singer almost cries and says, "*My Precious Jesus... without him... how lost I would be..*" And tears came to my eyes.

Lately, I have been listening to Beethoven and Bach while I clean my house. This background music is quiet, but it is heard by all. Somehow, my soul got weak and dry and tired. And I forgot about the joy and sorrowful happiness I get from listening to "Daddy's" old music.

Then I remembered my goal as a mother. I don't want my children remembering me as worldly, or even grumpy! I want them to remember me reading the Bible each day with a contented spirit. I want them to remember me listening to the old gospel songs and seeing the soaring faith from the look in my eyes.

Their memories of home. . *that will teach them. . .* those things cannot be conveyed in words. This kind of life is passed on from generation to generation, but only if we remember to make the effort to do the old tasks - the old religious duties.

Happy Homemaking

Today I put on my favorite skirt, my Edwardian Apron and my pearl necklace. I put my hair up and got to work on making a home. Our construction crew finished their work yesterday and now I am ready to put everything back in order.

I delighted in vacuuming and sweeping. My wood stove is now polished and tidy. Our living room looks inviting and lovely.

Mr. White went to the kitchen to get some coffee. He saw me Windex-ing and scrubbing my dustpan. He smiled and thought I was bizarre. (smiles). Doesn't everyone clean their dustpan after use?

I pulled out some beef to defrost for tonight's supper. I will make beef stew and biscuits.

In a little bit, I am going to make Ghiradelli chocolate chip cookies.

I am listening to my favorite gospel music and enjoying a precious day doing my housework.

Mozart Inspired Housekeeping

I just took down the burgundy curtains from my living room windows. I put them in the washing machine. Then I started to dust the blinds and ceiling. I am listening to Mozart's Chamber Music while I work. The living room looks spacious as I empty out the day's clutter. I am going to do a little rearranging and cleaning.

The room needs brightening!

Then I will work on polishing up the kitchen before the sun sets. Because once it gets dark, I only have limited lighting available - cozy dim lamps. The gentle light reflecting off the recently cleaned rooms will look charming and inviting.

I will have to create some sort of dinner plan. I will set the table in *thrifty elegance*. We will have a simple meal of chicken and potatoes. Then I will sit by the hearth and rest and read while my family runs off in many directions in this large old house, to pursue their own adventures.

Home in New England

It is a rainy, cool day up in the Vermont Mountains of New England. We are settled and cozy indoors. I had a hot cup of tea this morning. We have large windows at the front of our parlour and I can see the beautiful landscape with great picturesque clarity.

These cool spring days are pleasant. I am going to do a little cleaning this afternoon. Then I will settle down in my antique chair by the window and read for a bit. I am sure the phone will ring, and the children will need things. I am sure I will have to fix a mess or handle a crisis. But through it all, I will keep going back to my *little chair* and read. These will be my short breaks from life. It will be the quiet time of refreshment.

When the sun sets tonight, I will listen to Frank Sinatra in my kitchen, while I clean and tidy and polish and cook. I will wear my heels and my favorite apron. And I will set the mood for a happy home here in New England.

Acting Happy to Cheer Up

As I was working in my kitchen yesterday, one of my moods came on. (smiles) It was a somber, sad mood. Those things happen from time-to-time for no apparent reason. It is not pleasant. I tried everything I could think of to cheer up. I didn't want to alarm the family. I didn't want the children to see me sad. I knew if they were laughing and happy, it would gladden my heart. So I turned on some Christmas music and it helped tremendously.

Sometimes we just have to **act** happy, and wait for the *feeling* or *emotion* to follow. I cannot tell you how many times I've smiled, with a joyous glow in my eyes, and a warm remark to a child or stranger, despite some misery in my soul. It is not that I *hide* the occasional pain. It is more like pushing it away and refusing to let it overcome me. I cannot dwell on sadness.

Today, it is time to focus on spreading rainbows and happy thoughts. I will do a little housekeeping this morning. I will do some baking. I will listen to Christmas music and get dressed up. Then I will spend the day playing games with the children and reading them stories. I will be enchanted by whatever delights them!

It will be a lovely day!

Spiritual Duty of Mother

If Mother's daily - moment by moment delight was in spiritual matters: hymns, Bible, sermons, prayer; and this gave her great joy - don't you realize the serious impact this will have on the silent witnesses [her children] in her home?

Regardless of the spiritual state of those children, it *will* affect them.

It may not be seen now... or tomorrow... as we cannot watch a little plant grow in a day. We must wait as long as it takes for the *result*. God does not ask more of a parent who is hopelessly flawed.

Silence in the Morning Garden

I love getting up early in the morning and heading outside. The air is slightly cool. I can wear a shawl or sweater as I walk the property. *The world is asleep.* The sun has barely risen and I am enjoying the silence of a new day.

There is hope when I walk outdoors. I can pray and think and enjoy the beauty of my surroundings.

Perhaps I will pick some flowers and bring them inside. Perhaps I will have tea on the front porch and read. Such pleasant times in the morning.

It is a delight to be at home.

Housekeeping Despite Lack of Motivation

This is one of those days when I don't want to clean. I do not care for dusting, washing floors, sweeping, polishing counters or doing dishes. This is not a good mood for me. I cannot indulge it. I guess I am in a pampered mood and want to relax and be waited on. Yet, this will not happen, since I am the housekeeper.

I will have to make a list. The list will be my guide because my thoughts are not where they should be. You know how it says in the Bible that if we commit our works to the Lord, our thoughts will be established? (Proverbs 16:3) So I will make myself do the housework. After I cross several things off the dreaded list, I will start to enjoy myself. I realize this is just a mood I am in. It is a slacker mood. It is a terrible mood. I will have to work very hard to overcome it today.

Yet, I think I can motivate myself to work harder than normal. I will even wash the floors and clean the ashes from the wood stove. I will make things look lovely, until I *start* to feel lovely myself!

A Home Without Chaos

Some days I sense enough anxiety that I feel as if it will choke the life out of me. But this is what slows me down. This is what stops my busyness and takes me to a *precious state* of contented weariness.

It makes me yearn for a life of peace and happiness. And this anxiety helps make it happen.

Grandfathers and Grandmothers who have slowed down, and keep to a home routine are the most peaceful people I know. They have lived long lives and have experienced many things. Very few things surprise or startle them anymore. They smile knowingly and have the greatest amount of patience in anyone I've ever seen.

The home routine of the elderly goes at a slower pace. They are *not* rushing off to this event or that one. They have homes without chaos. This may seem difficult to replicate when there are little ones and teenagers with so many needs, but it can happen. It comes from the heart.

I have cut back on so many things that there is much time for leisure. This time of leisure makes me patient and loving and able to endure many things.

Those around us may have trials and troubles, but Mother's presence calms and soothes it all.

To have a home without chaos does not mean there is no trouble, for that would be a lonely, solitary place with no residents. This home I speak of, *the peaceful home*, comes from a soul weary mother who is heartsick for heaven. There is a joy in her demeanor that *quiets* onlookers.

Modern day troubles are nothing to her, because they are nothing to her God. She knows who is sovereign over all. She has great faith that He is in control. Why should she fret?

Her heartsickness makes her talk of the great journey she is slowly taking towards her eternal home. Why should she be caught up in the trials of this life? Her King will take care of that.

A precious, peaceful home is a state of mind. It is deliberate, but takes much effort. It can happen for those who are weary of this world's game. It starts with a mother of great faith, who knows to whom she belongs.

Do you see that heavenly light in the window? Do you see the peace and warmth in Mother? *She is the keeper of the home without chaos.* All who enter her house, despite what they see before them, are quickly comforted by the welcome of the heaven-bound mother.

Just a Regular Mom

I have been doing a little bit of reading today. I am seeing a lot of godly Mothers who are very busy at home. They seem to be doing it all. They are super organized, have home businesses, have great goals and accomplish them, have sweet looking children and are amazing.

But, you know what? I am exhausted reading about their lives, their teachings, their lessons and their devotions. I am tired.

I am just a regular mom. I live a quiet life. I love cleaning my house. I love making a home. I adore my children and I am grateful that they ALL adore me back. I have a 21 year old who still calls me "Mommy." I am happy in my quiet simple life. I do not have any ambitions. I have no strength for that. My children's home-education has consisted of the basics, and lots of Bible. They are all very hard working children who take care of me.

I was thinking today about the author, Elizabeth Prentiss. She was an amazing writer from the 1800's. (She actually lived in Vermont!) She was a minister's wife and the daughter of a minister. She wrote the most amazing, precious, spiritually nourishing books I have ever read in my life. These are all stories, fiction - but they are powerful lessons about having a godly, calm, peaceful home life.

In some of her books, there is always a much loved Mother or grandmother who adores her Bible and sits and reads. She is treasured by the characters in the books. She is a wise and much loved presence in the home. This "mother" has no ambition but to comfort and counsel her children. Her only daily task is to be with her family and to nurture them.

I want to be just like her...... I get glimpses of my future. My oldest girls, ages 20 and 21, have both told me that someday, whenever I want, they will provide me with a darling room in their own homes. They will take care of me and I will be a part of their own families. This is the regular mom, but it is a godly mom and that is who I aspire to be.

Some Quotes

"We Christians must simplify our lives or lose untold treasure on earth and in eternity. Modern civilization is so complex as to make the devotional life all but impossible. It wears us out by multiplying distractions and beats us down by destroying our solitude, where otherwise we might drink and renew our strength before going out to face the world again." (A.W. Tozer)

"Courtiers are more polite in their
manners than ordinary subjects,
because they are more in the prince's
eye and company.

The oftener we are in God's court,
the more holy shall we become."

-Thomas Manton [Puritan Minister]

"As we set about duty, God strengthens the influence that he has in us. We find a warmness of heart and increase of strength, the Spirit going along with us and raising us up by degrees, until he leaves us at it were in Heaven." - Richard Sibbes, 1630

"A home is an enclosure, a secret, separate place, a place shut in from, guarded against, the whole world outside. [The home is] "the peculiar sphere of woman. With the world at large, she has little to do. Her influence begins, centers, and ends in her home." - John F. Ware, 1800's.

For The Love of Christian Homemaking

The Mission House

A Wise Old Mother thought of her house as a mission. She craved the idea of being a missionary for the Lord. So she set about, making preparations.

First, she got rid of most of her worldly goods. She did not want to be overly attached to them, or tied - down by caring for them. She sold what she could, just like the Immigrants sold their household items to pay for their trip to a new land. Well, perhaps this mother took the money to pay off a few little debts, or maybe she gave it to charity.

Second, she organized her daily duties. She wanted to have a list of responsibilities. It was a like a job description for running the mission. These are some of the items on her list:

Morning tasks-

1. Chapel. (This consisted of Bible reading, prayer and the signing of hymns)

2. Prepare breakfast.

3. Clean kitchen.

4. Tidy parlour.

5. Handle correspondence and administrative duties.

Afternoon tasks -

1. Prepare Lunch.

2. Clean kitchen.

3. Do the household laundry.

4. Prayer and Rest.

Evening tasks -

1. Prepare Dinner.

2. Clean kitchen.

3. Chapel (This consisted of Bible reading, prayer and hymns.)

In the midst of all her daily work, she had to greet and welcome guests. She was to work right alongside them. Some of her guests found great delight in the daily labors of the mission house. They were able to talk with her, pray with her, and enjoy a bit of respite from the world.

She also had boarders to care for. These were of all ages, from babies to adults. She had full charge of their care and was quite busy with all their concerns and needs. She found this to be exhausting, but greatly rewarding. She was honored with the "burden," and felt privileged to have them staying with her.

At other times of the day, she would be called away on a mission errand. She was to dress accordingly, knowing she represented the mission house. She had to be an ambassador of that important work and had to be pleasant to all she met. She had grace and dignity and an incredibly strong spirit.

Sometimes, she would walk the grounds of the mission house and enjoy some peaceful quiet, alone with the Lord. This made up for when her time with the Lord was an almost never-ending conversation with the Master of the Mission house - These were prayers and thanksgivings and praises that could not be uttered because of the overflowing joy in her heart.

Last of all, she worked through weariness and became stronger. She worked even when no visible results came from her efforts. She worked and worked and worked, at the Mission House, and made it a shining example of a resting place for weary souls.

But the secret to her motivation was one quiet morning, as she read this dear quote from a group of "real" missionaries, as they struggled to do God's work in foreign lands:

"O Lord," they had prayed, "Send revival. . and let it start in me."

Index

(Includes the date each post was originally written)

For The Love of Christian Homemaking

For The Love of Christian Homemaking

For The Love of Christian Homemaking

About the Author

Mrs. White is the granddaughter of revival preacher, LD Murphy. She is the founder of "The Legacy of Home" blog, which encourages mothers to have peaceful, godly homes.

Mrs. White and her husband are natives of New England. They have 5 older children and 2 grandchildren, and have been homeschooling for more than 20 years. They currently live in an old 1800's house in rural Vermont.

Visit Mrs. White at

http://thelegacyofhome.blogspot.com

Made in the USA
Middletown, DE
04 September 2021